TEDDINGTON
A HISTORY & CELEBRATION

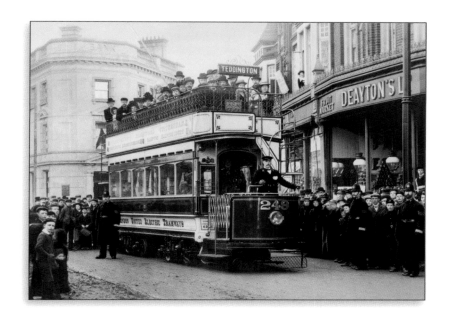

DR ANDREW HOLT

Andrew Holt

THE FRANCIS FRITH COLLECTION

www.francisfrith.co.uk

First published in the United Kingdom in 2005
by The Francis Frith Collection®

Hardback Edition 2005
ISBN 1-84589-219-4

British Library Cataloguing in Publication Data

Teddington - A History & Celebration
Dr Andrew Holt

The Francis Frith Collection
Frith's Barn, Teffont,
Salisbury, Wiltshire SP3 5QP
Tel: +44 (0) 1722 716 376
Email: info@francisfrith.co.uk
www.francisfrith.co.uk

Printed and bound in England

Front Cover: **TEDDINGTON, A FIRST-DAY TRAM IN BROAD STREET**
        1903 ZZZ05516t (Graham Sims Collection)

Additional modern photographs by Tom Holt and Vicky Higgins
unless otherwise specified.

Domesday extract used in timeline by kind permission of
Alecto Historical Editions, www.domesdaybook.org
Aerial photographs reproduced under licence from
Simmons Aerofilms Limited.
Historical Ordnance Survey maps reproduced under licence from
Homecheck.co.uk

Every attempt has been made to contact copyright holders of
illustrative material. We will be happy to give full acknowledgement in
future editions for any items not credited. Any information should be
directed to The Francis Frith Collection.

*The colour-tinting in this book is for illustrative purposes only,
and is not intended to be historically accurate*

CONTENTS

TEDDINGTON FROM THE AIR AF23399

TEDDINGTON
A HISTORY & CELEBRATION

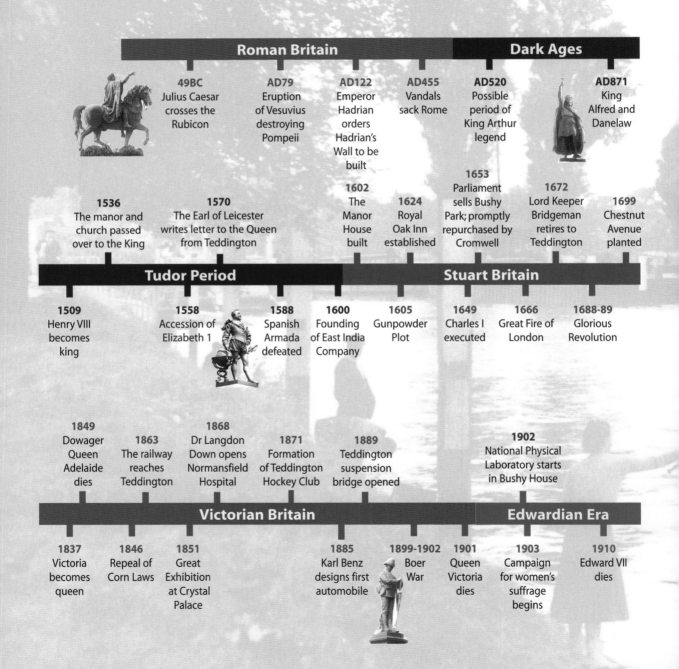

Roman Britain

49BC Julius Caesar crosses the Rubicon

AD79 Eruption of Vesuvius destroying Pompeii

AD122 Emperor Hadrian orders Hadrian's Wall to be built

AD455 Vandals sack Rome

Dark Ages

AD520 Possible period of King Arthur legend

AD871 King Alfred and Danelaw

1536 The manor and church passed over to the King

1570 The Earl of Leicester writes letter to the Queen from Teddington

1602 The Manor House built

1624 Royal Oak Inn established

1653 Parliament sells Bushy Park; promptly repurchased by Cromwell

1672 Lord Keeper Bridgeman retires to Teddington

1699 Chestnut Avenue planted

Tudor Period

Stuart Britain

1509 Henry VIII becomes king

1558 Accession of Elizabeth 1

1588 Spanish Armada defeated

1600 Founding of East India Company

1605 Gunpowder Plot

1649 Charles I executed

1666 Great Fire of London

1688-89 Glorious Revolution

1849 Dowager Queen Adelaide dies

1863 The railway reaches Teddington

1868 Dr Langdon Down opens Normansfield Hospital

1871 Formation of Teddington Hockey Club

1889 Teddington suspension bridge opened

1902 National Physical Laboratory starts in Bushy House

Victorian Britain

Edwardian Era

1837 Victoria becomes queen

1846 Repeal of Corn Laws

1851 Great Exhibition at Crystal Palace

1885 Karl Benz designs first automobile

1899-1902 Boer War

1901 Queen Victoria dies

1903 Campaign for women's suffrage begins

1910 Edward VII dies

HISTORICAL TIMELINE FOR TEDDINGTON

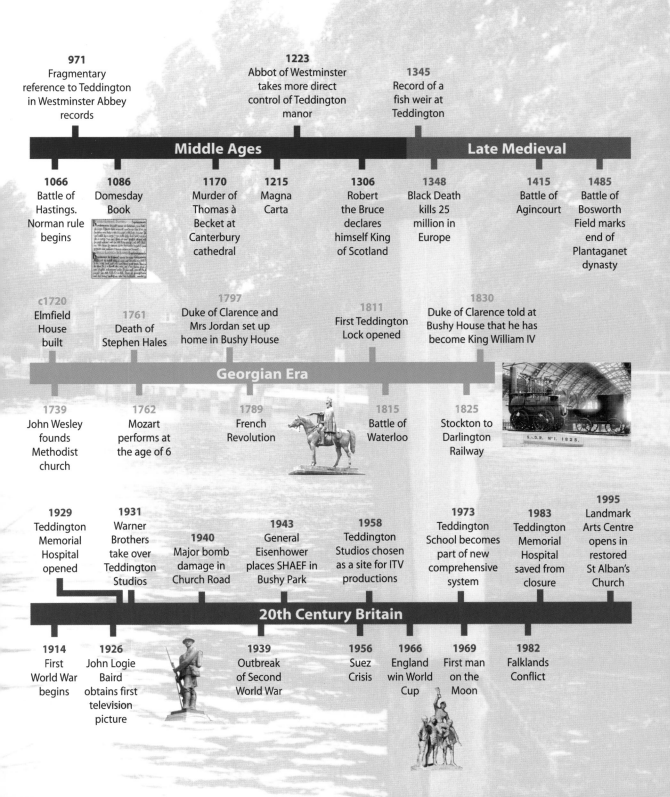

971
Fragmentary reference to Teddington in Westminster Abbey records

1223
Abbot of Westminster takes more direct control of Teddington manor

1345
Record of a fish weir at Teddington

Middle Ages

Late Medieval

1066
Battle of Hastings. Norman rule begins

1086
Domesday Book

1170
Murder of Thomas à Becket at Canterbury cathedral

1215
Magna Carta

1306
Robert the Bruce declares himself King of Scotland

1348
Black Death kills 25 million in Europe

1415
Battle of Agincourt

1485
Battle of Bosworth Field marks end of Plantaganet dynasty

c1720
Elmfield House built

1761
Death of Stephen Hales

1797
Duke of Clarence and Mrs Jordan set up home in Bushy House

1811
First Teddington Lock opened

1830
Duke of Clarence told at Bushy House that he has become King William IV

Georgian Era

1739
John Wesley founds Methodist church

1762
Mozart performs at the age of 6

1789
French Revolution

1815
Battle of Waterloo

1825
Stockton to Darlington Railway

1929
Teddington Memorial Hospital opened

1931
Warner Brothers take over Teddington Studios

1940
Major bomb damage in Church Road

1943
General Eisenhower places SHAEF in Bushy Park

1958
Teddington Studios chosen as a site for ITV productions

1973
Teddington School becomes part of new comprehensive system

1983
Teddington Memorial Hospital saved from closure

1995
Landmark Arts Centre opens in restored St Alban's Church

20th Century Britain

1914
First World War begins

1926
John Logie Baird obtains first television picture

1939
Outbreak of Second World War

1956
Suez Crisis

1966
England win World Cup

1969
First man on the Moon

1982
Falklands Conflict

CHAPTER ONE
RURAL TEDDINGTON

FOR MUCH of its existence Teddington has been regarded as a quiet town between the busier Richmond, Twickenham and Kingston centres on the River Thames. Nationally it may be best remembered as the home of Teddington Studios, the location for films and TV productions. However, Teddington's proximity to London and its pleasant surroundings has attracted some significant residents. Also, Teddington is where one king learnt of his accession to the throne; it is the home of the National Physical Laboratory; it is where D-Day was planned; and the game of hockey started here.

The name Teddington is Saxon in origin, and referred to the small village in the area close to the river covering what is now Teddington Lock, the nearby church buildings of St Mary and St Alban, and the river end of Teddington High Street. The wider area now regarded as Teddington, stretching from the river through Bushy Park, Fulwell and Waldegrave Road, was countryside - a mix of heathland and forest. Hampton Wick was a separate village connected by road. This basically rural environment remained until well into the 19th century.

While continuous settlement in Teddington started in Saxon times, there had been significant human activity in the Stone Age: flints have been discovered in the dredging of the Thames. A major Bronze Age barrow was excavated in 1854 where Sandy Lane comes close to the railway. It stood twelve feet high, and there were a few remains; a dagger had survived, and fragments of a large half-baked urn and some calcified bones were also found. The mound disappeared with the construction of the railway in the 1860s.

THE THAMES AT TEDDINGTON 1899 43048

Although Roman artefacts have been discovered, there was no substantial Roman site here. Nor do exact records exist of when continuous Saxon settlement started in Teddington or when the first church was built. Upstream on the other side of the river was the well-developed Kingston community, where some of the Saxon kings were crowned. The original inhabitants of Teddington may have 'spun off' from Kingston, or may simply have migrated from Hounslow Heath. Although Teddington is not specifically mentioned in the Domesday Book, there are sufficient fragmentary references to indicate that a Teddington village existed by the first millennium and developed during the subsequent centuries.

Fact File

Tides and Names

As a river on the eastern side of England, the Thames flows through receding land. In Roman times, the tides hardly reached London. By the 12th century they had reached Kingston and beyond, possibly as far as Staines on occasion. Teddington, Todyngton, Tutington and other variants for the name of the village in Saxon and Norman times certainly did not stand for 'Tide-End-Town' as has often been suggested.

Under Saxon administration the lands surrounding Teddington were part of the Middlesex shire, with Surrey on the opposite bank (a distinction that has remained until this day in postal district terms). These lands fell within the Spelthorne Hundred, which stretched along the river to Staines. In Roman times Staines - or Ad Pontens by its Roman name - was a significant military base and township, and the Saxons built upon its remains in the Dark Ages. So when Teddington was placed under the Abbey of Westminster by the first Saxon Christian kings, it was initially administered by monks in Staines. In 1223, following some disputes, this was altered to more direct rule from the Abbey of Westminster in terms of the appointment of the curate and maintenance.

As a consequence of ecclesiastical rule, there are records for the late medieval period. In her booklet '14th-Century Medieval Teddington', Mary Clarke brings out the structure and daily life of the village. The feudal manorial system was in place. The manor itself held a significant portion of the cultivated land and animals. The population of between 100 and 200 people was a mix of tenants with their own strips of land and animals, along with freemen, and some servants providing direct labour to the manor. Tenants paid rent and were committed to working the manor fields for a number of days in the year, particularly at harvest and other peak periods. There were also tasks to do with the maintenance of the manor house and equipment, some particular occupations such as swineherd and shepherd, and the more occasional need for specialists such as locksmiths, carpenters and thatchers. The river was used for fishing and as a means of transport for the exchange of animals with other villages. The abbots were absentee landlords, with visiting bailiffs acting on their behalf. The reeve, elected by the tenants, was the main administrator and the key figure, with some power that may not always have been scrupulously deployed. Some of Teddington's reeves held their office for long periods, which may suggest trustworthiness.

Although the Hundred Years' War added to the tax burden, Teddington was unaffected by the main political events of the time. In contrast, the major catastrophe of the century hit hard. The Black Death plague of 1349-50 and another wave in 1361 are estimated to have taken over 20% of the population of England, and some academics suggest it may have been in the 30-40% region. The plague struck indiscriminately at the ruling clergy at Westminster and the villagers, at males and females, and at adults and children, even if in Teddington it may not have reached the devastating levels implied by the overall numbers for England. Apart from the immediate sorrow and practical difficulties, the economic impact was severe for the manor thanks to lost rents, the higher cost of labour, and the lack of care for animals and fields. However, as elsewhere, there was an economic recovery; by the end of the century the land under cultivation had expanded, there were improvements in the quality of buildings, and new breeds of animals had appeared. There are no physical remains from this period, but the chapel was sited where St Mary's Church now stands, and the basic geography of Teddington village was set; roads ran along the river to Twickenham in one direction and to Hampton Wick in the other, and the High Street led away from the river towards Hounslow. A fish weir was in place, and among the new animals were swans - later to become an emblem of Teddington.

Tudor times were more eventful. The construction of Hampton Court, its 'presentation' by Cardinal Wolsey to Henry VIII in 1525, the divorce and second marriage of the king, and Anne Boleyn's residency at the new royal palace meant that some of the major political events of the time were played out close to Teddington. The associated Reformation changed the ownership of land and churches. And with royalty coming and going regularly, there came extra traffic and the requirement to support the court.

For the village of Teddington, the main changes concerned the church and the manor. The basic design of St Mary's Church as we know it today was established in its reconstruction during this period, and the southern aisle has survived. Robert Feron, the priest at Teddington, was indicted in 1535 for 'treasonable' criticisms of the king's church policies alongside a priest from Isleworth and others, but he was saved (possibly by turning king's evidence), while his colleagues

THE SWAN AND STAG
EDITED BY DUDLEY W. WALTON, F.S.S.

THE SWAN EMBLEM 1925 ZZZ05466
(Richmond upon Thames Local Studies Collection)

A SWAN ON THE RIVER AT TEDDINGTON 2005 T19701k (Vicky Higgin)

Swans first appeared in England in the late 12th or early 13th century and reached Teddington in the 14th century. Ownership had to be licensed by the Crown.

THE WEIR 1890 23539

This was a long-term successor of the original weir.

were executed. The Abbot of Westminster handed over the manor, church and lands to the King in 1536. The villagers and their priests seem to have survived the 1550s shifts from Protestant to Catholic and back to Protestant without major alarums or martyrs. Henry VIII's successors acquired more land during the remainder of the century but, unlike neighbouring Hampton and Twickenham, the manor held on to it through to the 19th century.

With kings and queens come courts and the need for entertainment, including hunting and other outdoor sports. These were available in the lands away from the river at Hampton Court, which were to be put at the disposal of the monarchs and their courtiers. The process had started before the construction of Hampton Court Palace, with the enclosure of land in Hampton in 1500 and its stocking with wild deer (and as a result preserved the medieval field

system which can still be seen today). After the construction of Hampton Court Palace the process of enclosing land to create a larger area for hunting and other outdoor court entertainment was accelerated. The Teddington lands were among the earlier ones to be absorbed into what became known as Bushy Park. By 1620 the park had the boundaries we know today. The first walls went up around 1540, but the individual parts of the park were still separated, and it was well into the 18th century before it became one park and was fully walled. There was a major risk to the park's continued existence during the Commonwealth period when Parliament sold the land in 1653 on the grounds that the activities in the park were not consistent with the aspirations of sober puritan life. Fortunately, Cromwell was living in Hampton Court, and he promptly bought the park back, so it survived into the Restoration.

HAMPTON COURT, THE DEER IN BUSHY PARK c1960 H17053

THE CREATION OF CHESTNUT AVENUE

The mile-long avenue between Teddington and Hampton Court, flanked by lines of lime and chestnut trees, is the most famous feature of Bushy Park. It started as part of a grand scheme that was never fully implemented. William III had planned to bring the Tudor Hampton Court up to date with the grand, classical designs of the late 17th century. Sir Christopher Wren's idea was to make the approach to the upgraded palace a wide avenue starting at the Teddington gate, running through the park across the road, and ending at the front of the palace, with any intervening walls and gates demolished. Another avenue was to meet it at right angles roughly half way down, where the Longford river would have crossed it. The lime trees were planted in 1689, and the chestnut trees in 1699. The basin for the pond, where the two avenues were to meet, was also laid down. At that point William III had a riding accident, and died within two weeks of it. His successor, Queen Anne, was not interested in furthering the project, and it was brought to a close with the completion of the avenue to the Hampton Court gate and its termination there, leaving the Lion Gate as the only visible part of Hampton Court from the Teddington side. The crossing avenue had been cleared on the west side down to Hampton Hill and was kept, but the eastern avenue had hardly been started and was left to peter out. The bronze statue on top of the fountain in the middle of the pond is of Arethusa - the pedestal is white marble. The fountain was moved in 1713 from the King's Privy Garden, where it could be viewed close up; its subtlety is rather lost in the middle of the large pond. The name Diana Fountain emerged later, but the reasons for the change are obscure, and have been a subject of debate and confusion. Apart from the upgrading of the road to take modern traffic, the avenue running between the lines of almost 1,000 trees in total remains as it was left in 1699. The weather has sometimes damaged it. The storm of 1703 did not have lasting impact, as the trees were still young. However, the whirlwind storm of 1908, the hurricane of 1987, and the subsequent storm in 1989 destroyed many trees. Felling and replanting had to be done, with recovery taking over a decade.

THE DIANA FOUNTAIN, BUSHY PARK c2000
ZZZ05467 (Courtesy of the Royal Parks)

HAMPTON COURT, THE LION GATES c1960 H17067

In the 17th and 18th centuries Teddington attracted some influential residents, thanks to the presence of royalty, the patronage of the keepers of Bushy Park, and the fact that the town was only two hours' ride from London. While some of the royal appointees (such as Sir Amias Poulet, the man made responsible for the keeping of Mary, Queen of Scots in imprisonment) simply held the title of Lord of the Manor of Teddington, other appointees became residents, and some of these were active in the community.

The most senior political resident of Teddington in the 17th century was Sir Orlando Bridgeman. Born in Exeter and educated at Cambridge, he was called to the bar in 1632 and rose rapidly, becoming the solicitor-general to the future Charles II by 1640. During the Civil War he was involved in various treaty negotiations on behalf of the Royalists; he lived quietly in the country in the Commonwealth period. He reappeared with the Restoration, and advanced through the legal battles of the 1660s to become the Keeper of the Seal (the equivalent of today's Lord Chancellor) in 1667. He subsequently fell out of favour in court intrigues over finance and his opposition to the King's more indulgent approach to Catholics, and was dismissed in 1672. He retired to Teddington, where he was active in the provision for and maintenance of the church until his death in 1674. He was buried in St Mary's Church. His embalmed body was discovered during one of the 19th-century reconstructions of the church, much to the astonishment of the vicar of the day. His wife, who was influential and had been

regarded as difficult at court, continued to live in Teddington until her death 20 years later. She left £40 to the parish; this funded the first school in Teddington, with places for twelve girls. On the south side of the High Street, Bridgeman House carried their name and survived as home to St Alban's Club until well into the 20th century. It was demolished and later replaced by the BT building in 1951 (regarded by many as the worst break in the architecture of the current High Street). Although one reference to him was lost with the merger of Bridgeman Infants School into Collis School in 1981, Lord Keeper Bridgeman is still remembered by the names assigned to Bridgeman Road near the station, Orlando Cottage among the Peg Woffington cottages, Orlando Square on the railway bridge, and the wall monument and window to him in the church.

THE LORD BRIDGEMAN WINDOW 2005 ZZZ05468
(Courtesy of St Mary's Church, Teddington)

Probably the most distinguished resident of Teddington was Dr Stephen Hales. Born in 1677, he followed a clerical academic path at Cambridge; yet his interest in science was already established, with particular regard for the work of Isaac Newton and sound experimental method. He became parish priest for Teddington in 1709, and held the position for the rest of his life.

As a scientist, he took forward the study of blood circulation (he is regarded as a founder of haematology) and established the medical importance of blood pressure. During his work on this topic he discovered a new line of research. 'I was endeavoring to stop the bleeding of an old stem of a vine, which was cut too near to the bleeding season, which I feared might kill it'. He found that the sap pressure in the vine was several times that of the central artery of a horse or dog. Applying similar methods to measurement of the flow of sap across a wide range of vegetables, trees and vines, he created the science of plant physiology. He even applied his approach to the study of how the bones of chicken grow. The experimental methods he used were very cruel - he worked with un-anaesthetised animals - and the arguments of the poet Alexander Pope, who lived in Twickenham, persuaded him to stop for a while. He resumed after convincing himself that the pain to animals was outweighed by the benefits of his discoveries to humans. At a practical level, his interests in the circulation of air led him into the field of ventilation; machines were designed carrying forward his ideas, and these machines had an impressive impact

STEPHEN HALES 1759 ZZZ05469
(Courtesy of the National Portrait Gallery, London)

on the reduction of death rates in crowded spaces such as ships, hospitals, workhouses and prisons. He became active in promoting their use in the French wars of the 1750s, when he hoped that his correspondence with Louis XV on behalf of English prisoners of war would not be regarded as unpatriotic.

For his parishioners, his philosophy and sermons preached a Christianity that was benign. Nevertheless, observing the problems that the availability of cheap gin created, he was hard on excess consumption of hard liquor, and published a paper entitled 'Admonition to Drinkers of Brandy and Distilled Spirits'. Illegitimate children were common in Teddington; although not generally severe, Hales occasionally ordered public penance for transgression from the rules of the time for relationships between the sexes. He was responsible for the expansion of the church and its graveyard, and the 18th-century north aisle has survived subsequent reconstructions. A cupola was added to the bell tower on his instructions, and the old bells were replaced by a new one so that it could be better heard by parishioners. Later in his period as curate the wooden bell tower was replaced by a brick one. The most ambitious of his efforts for the parish was the provision of a new drainage system parallel to the High Street, using his measurements for the correct flow of water from the pond situated near where the station stands today. Although this deteriorated after his death, its basic design remained until the construction of the railway in the 1860s cut across it.

ST MARY'S CHURCH 1899 43551

ST MARY'S CHURCH 1899 43055

He was a straightforward and relatively simple man without any ambition for advancement. He became a Fellow of the Royal Society in 1719, received the prestigious Copley Medal in 1739, and was elected to the French Academy in 1753. By the 1750s his fame had grown, and his celebrity status attracted visitors. Frederick, the Prince of Wales, who was personally interested in science, made visits, and later Hales became chaplain to the Princess Dowager of Wales for a time. He was scientifically active into his eighties, still considering subjects such as the intensity of salt in sea-water and whether salt water would cleanse the body more thoroughly than other water. He died in 1761 and was buried at the church in Teddington. The memorial and tombstone are immediately in front on entry to the church today. The Princess Dowager funded a monument to him in Westminster Abbey.

> Beneath is the grave of Stephen Hales. The epitaph, now partly obliterated but recovered from a record of 1795, is here inscribed by the piety of certain Botanists. A.D. 1911:—
> Here is interr'd the Body of
> STEPHEN HALES, D.D.,
> Clerk of the Closet to the Princess of Wales, who was Minister of this Parish 51 years.
> He died the 4th. of January 1761 in the 84th. year of his age

THE MEMORIAL STONE TO STEPHEN HALES
ZZZ05470 (Courtesy of St Mary's Church, Teddington)

The Keepers of Bushy Park in the 17th and 18th centuries included a groom of the king's bedchamber, a chancellor of the exchequer, and the wife of a prime minister. Their different careers illustrate the capriciousness of political life. The first of these, Edward Proger, was a colourful figure. A page to Charles I, he rose to the position of solicitor to the Prince of Wales by 1640, and advanced to other support roles. He followed the prince into exile; later he was involved in trips across the Channel to further various plots, and was occasionally imprisoned. He was rewarded at the Restoration. His role appears to have been that of a 'fixer', and his duties with regard to the bedchamber included dealing with Charles II's mistresses and other intrigues.

He became keeper of part of Bushy Park in 1665; after his retirement from the court at the accession of James II, who had no need for his type of service, he resided in Bushy Park until his death at the age of 92, which was attributed to a strange cause - infection in his wisdom teeth.

His successor as keeper, George Montagu, Earl of Halifax, had a rapid rise, and became Chancellor of the Exchequer and Leader of the House in the 1690s. He transformed fiscal management. By raising a loan of £1million he started the National Debt; he set up the Bank of England; and he reorganised the operation of the Royal Mint (with his friend Isaac Newton in charge of the operation) as part of a successful effort to stabilise the currency in an inflationary period. In many respects he was the first modern chancellor of the exchequer. He ran into difficulties over alleged personal gain, and although he survived impeachment and other attacks in the first decade of the 18th century, his political career went into decline. He acquired a keepership of Bushy Park in 1709, and, on the death of Edward Proger, he was able to unify the keeperships into one position, which remained with the family until 1770.

Lord North's life was an illustration of the dictum that the end of political careers is generally failure. Born in 1732, he entered Parliament in 1754 and was Chancellor by 1767. He held office as Prime Minister (or First Lord Of the Treasury, as it was then called) from 1770 to 1782. Despite some successes in finance and skill in handling crises over India and Canada, he will always go down in history as the man who presided over the loss of the American colonies. His connection with Bushy Park started in 1771, when King George III wanted to reward him with the Keepership; because he was Prime Minister, the position had to be granted to Lady North. The Norths used Bushy House as for their summer residence, particularly after Lord North's retirement, which seemed a happy one. 'Lord North's spirit, good humour, wit, sense, drollery are as perfect as ever ... if the loss of sight could be compensated it is by so affectionate a family', wrote Horace Walpole (the youngest son of Robert Walpole, the first Prime Minister, and 18th-century author and prolific letter writer who lived in Strawberry Hill) after a visit.

Proger was a diligent keeper of Bushy Park during his long period there. Following a commission from King Charles II, he built Bushy House. This was done largely, and uncharacteristically, from his own pocket, and the Treasury never properly recompensed him. Under the Halifax family, Bushy House was rebuilt and extended with new wings. In the earlier years they tended to live in Upper Lodge to the west of Bushy House, and they reconstructed it as part of the agreement to secure the keepership. Formal gardens were added to Upper Lodge, which included a cascade between two ponds - they became well known, and attracted artists. There was a dispute over the public's right to cross Chestnut Avenue; this was eventually settled in favour of the public, who gained the right to use Cobbler's Walk running across the park from Hampton Wick. It was named after the occupation of Tim Bennett, under whose name the case had been pursued.

UPPER LODGE, BUSHY PARK c1775 ZZZ05471 (Richmond upon Thames Local Studies Collection)

By the end of the 18th century the main Teddington village had grown. It extended from the river down the High Street to a pond opposite Waldegrave Road (which was now a recognized road leaving Teddington), and some smaller houses had appeared in the Park Road area and towards the Bushy Park gate. The manor had leased some of the land on which wealthier residents built some substantial houses. Most of these were along the High Street. On the south side they included Teddington Place near the river (built with elegant internal decoration by Sir Charles Duncombe, a successful financier and Mayor of London in the early 18th century), Udney House by Kingston Lane (named after the wealthy merchant who lived there, who had a fine picture collection stemming from a period as Consul to Leghorn, which prompted a visit by King George III), and Bridgeman House. On the north side the manor house stood opposite the church, and there were three large houses near Waldegrave Road. Just one of these remains intact: Elmfield House, on the corner of Waldegrave Road, was acquired by the council in 1895 and is currently used as offices.

THE DRAWING ROOM, UDNEY HOUSE 1883 ZZZ05472 (Richmond upon Thames Local Studies Collection)

Although taken a century after the Udneys lived here, the print gives some idea of the interior of the house in their time.

To the north of the manor house, Grove House (designed by the eminent architect Sir William Chambers) was built for Mr Franks, a member of a small Jewish community. His successor in the house was John Walter, the founder of The Times newspaper. He had started working life in the 1750s as a coal merchant, and subsequently moved on, disastrously, to insurance underwriting, leaving him with debts that were not cleared until the 1790s. By then he had become involved in printing, deploying a new 'logographical' technique that used whole words rather than letter by letter production, which was speedier. He set up The Daily Universal Register newspaper in 1785, which became The Times in the 1790s. The paper ran into political trouble for criticizing the royal dukes, and John Walter was fined and suffered imprisonment. He took up residence in Grove House in 1795. He gradually let his son of the same name take over responsibility for the newspaper, and it was his son who took it to its full national status. He pursued a legal case against the churchwardens for not granting him a pew as a principal resident of the parish because his Jewish predecessor had not needed one. He won it in the end, but was not awarded costs. He then became very active in the church, and died in 1812. He was buried in the church graveyard, and there is a memorial stone to him on the northern wall inside the church. Grove House was demolished in the early 20th century.

As Paddy Ching indicates in her books on Teddington's houses, more of the houses along Park Road from this period remain, albeit with some modifications. These include Nos 22 (The Elms), 24, and 26 (Norfolk House, which is reached along a small lane), Park House at No 106 on the west side of the road, and Bushy Park Cottage at the corner on the east side opposite Bushy Park.

NORFOLK LODGE COACH HOUSE, PARK ROAD 2005 T19704k (Tom Holt)

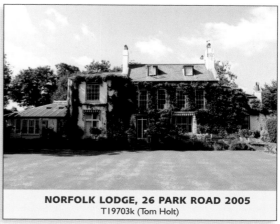

NORFOLK LODGE, 26 PARK ROAD 2005 T19703k (Tom Holt)

Both Norfolk House and the coach house probably originate from the 18th century, with modifications since. The coach house has been brought into domestic use recently.

14 AND 16 PARK ROAD 2005
T19702k (Vicky Higgin)

Clarence Cottage to the right is 18th-century, but Adelaide Cottage to the left is early 19th-century; at one time the two were adjoined as a common house.

The village population had grown to just short of 700, and there were now over 100 houses. The way of life had remained basically agricultural. This was the period of 'the Little Ice Age', when there were severe winters and the Thames frequently froze over, so farming life was hard. New occupations had appeared, such as butcher, shoemaker, blacksmith, and bricklayer, and there were opportunities for domestic service in the wealthier residents' houses. A wax bleaching and candle making factory was in operation on Waldegrave Road, which provided further jobs. There were three pubs - the Royal Oak and the King's Head on the High Street, roughly where their namesakes are today, and the Clarence Arms (now the Park Hotel) on Park Road. The community had its poor, who were covered by church donations and the parish almshouses. Receipt of charity

was not always easy, and the willingness to provide it was already tempered with the stern attitudes that framed the Poor Laws of the Victorian era. Sometimes the recipients of charity had to wear badges; there were restrictions on owning dogs; and poorhouses and workhouses were often the destination of applicants (the Teddington parish tended to use Hampton and Kingston facilities rather than build their own). Vagrant control was regarded as important to deal with itinerant beggars, many of whom died in miserable conditions, particularly women in childbirth.

THE KING'S HEAD, HIGH STREET 2005 T19705k
(Tom Holt)

The King's Head has been in existence since the 17th century. It was used until 1865 for the Court Leets in which the manor owner settled outstanding matters with tenants. Today, much modified, it hosts a French restaurant at the front with a traditional pub and gardens at the rear.

PEG WOFFINGTON AND THE COTTAGE

Born in Ireland, Peg Woffington began her stage career in Dublin; in the 1740s and 1750s she was the most celebrated actress of the day, appearing with great success in a variety of roles in Dublin and in London. Her connection with Teddington started with the purchase of 'a lovely villa' near the river (we cannot be certain which one it was) which she used from 1744. She often performed alongside the actor David Garrick, who later erected a villa on the river at Hampton which still stands today. The end of her career was dramatic. She collapsed on stage in the fifth act of 'As You Like It' (acting Rosalind) in 1756; although she survived, she remained in poor health until her death in 1760. The traditional story is that she spent much of that time in Teddington, and funded the erection of the cottages that bear her name for use by the poor. Doubt has been cast on this, and the evidence is mostly against it. What is definite is that she died in London, was buried in Teddington, and a memorial to her can be seen in St Mary's Church. Guests at the cottage tearoom can also be assured that they are consuming their lunches and cream teas in a cottage 250 years old.

PEG WOFFINGTON'S COTTAGE, HIGH STREET 2005 ZZZ05519 (Tony Mansell)

External security was a preoccupation; in the 18th century there were six gates across the roads into the village, manned by the poor for small sums of money. Three of these were on the main roads - the ones to Twickenham and Hampton Wick by the river, and on the Hampton Road at what is now Broad Street. There is uncertainty over the location of the others, with Watts Lane, Kingston Lane, and Waldegrave Road the favourite guesses. The wide area of Hounslow Heath on the north side of the village was not safe at night,

and a number of robberies occurred here. Relations with other villages were not always smooth. The most serious incident was a 'maypole fight' in 1710: there was a fight with visiting men from Twickenham in which a Teddington man died. The parish dealt with minor crimes committed within the village. The stocks had been used as a form of punishment, but were in decay in the 18th century; they were replaced by a 'round house or parish cage for punishment of disorderly persons'.

A CATTLE TROUGH ON PARK ROAD 2005 T19706k (Vicky Higgin)

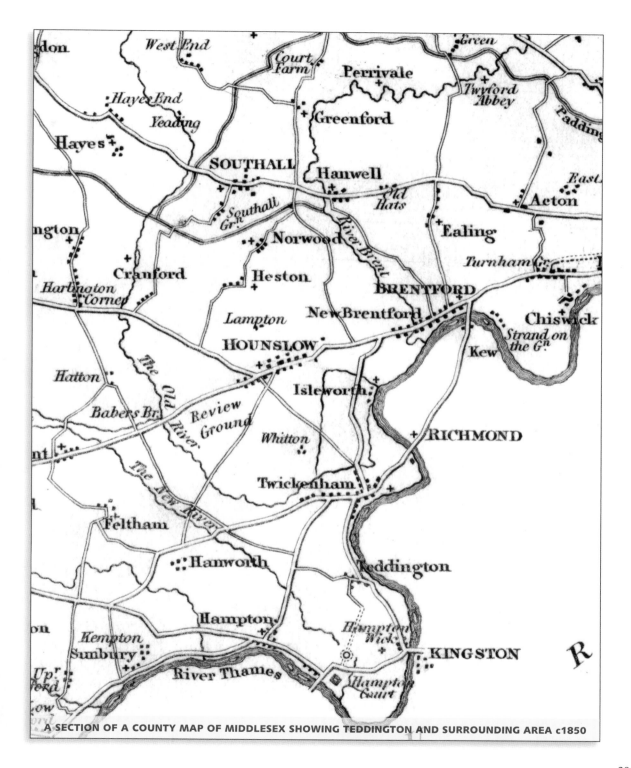

A SECTION OF A COUNTY MAP OF MIDDLESEX SHOWING TEDDINGTON AND SURROUNDING AREA c1850

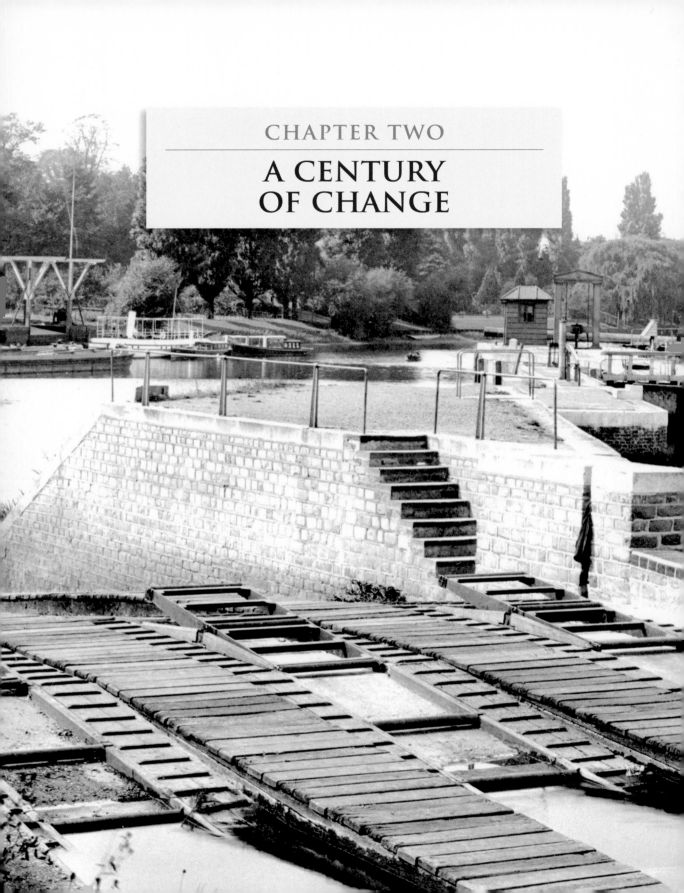

CHAPTER TWO

A CENTURY
OF CHANGE

TWO REMINISCENCES from the standpoint of the early 20th century bring the scale of change in the 19th century to life. The first recalls a boy flying a kite in Bushy Park being approached by a tall gentleman and told: 'You must not fly your kite here'. After the boy answered a few questions, the gentleman changed his mind and said that the boy could continue flying his kite and that he should ignore anyone who tried to stop him, as he had the permission of the park's owner. The gentleman was the owner - none other than the future King William IV. The second recalls a Teddington village with just one butcher, two grocers, two bakers and general stores that together supplied the needs of the community, a village pond with lilacs and ducks, and plenty of surrounding cornfields.

KING WILLIAM IV 1830 ZZZ05527
(Courtesy of the National Portrait Gallery, London)

The world of the Hanoverian monarchs and a small rural village were very remote from the suburbs those who were remembering the past now lived in, with railway and tram transport, a population that had multiplied more than tenfold, and continuous housing along many of the streets.

The presence of royalty stemmed from one of the scandals of the late 18th century. William IV was the third son of George III. He was never expected to become king, and his father designated a naval career for him. He first set off to sea in 1779 at the age of thirteen, and for the subsequent decade experienced many of the features of the naval life of the time - long spells at sea, periods in remote places such as the coast of Newfoundland, minor naval battles, drunken parties, transient relationships with women, and whorehouses. He ran up substantial debts, so he was relieved when, after ending his naval career, he was made Duke of Clarence in 1789 with a higher income that enabled him to set up on his own in London away from the court.

In common with his siblings, he was subject to the Royal Marriages Act, under which he could not marry without the king's permission. The Act had been conceived by George III as a means of preventing undesirable marriages for his children. It proved a most counter-productive measure. His sons developed long-term relationships with 'unsuitable' women, or led profligate lives alongside nominal marriages. This was partly responsible for the low reputation of the monarchy in the public's eyes, and provided fertile grounds for critical press coverage that makes the treatment of problems within the current House of Windsor look muted. In William's case, being restricted to the Protestant princesses of Northern Europe was not appealing; after some temporary liaisons, he became attracted to the most famous actress of the day - Mrs Jordan.

MRS JORDAN 1791 ZZZ05529 (Courtesy of the Tate Gallery, on loan to the National Portrait Gallery, London)

Dorothy Jordan was born in Ireland and started her career there. The poor state of that country at the time forced her to look to England to advance her career and make ends meet. After some years on the Yorkshire theatrical circuit she transferred to London, and had great success in all types of roles

at Covent Garden and Drury Lane in the 1780s. She had had unfortunate experiences with two theatrical managers, and had three living children by them. It took 11 months of courtship before William finally secured his prize in 1790. The new royal liaison provided the press with great material to attack the monarchy, and they did so with vigour.

William and Mrs Jordan settled down as what would now be termed 'partners' for 20 years. It was in many ways a modern relationship: she continued her successful career and provided a substantial portion of the income of the household. Although the relationship was deemed scandalous to begin with, its longevity and the appearance of ten children brought most people's acceptance, including the king's (but not the queen's). On the death of Lady North, King George III awarded the Keepership of Bushy Park to William in 1797. The couple set up home in Bushy House. Here there were few interruptions to a happy and settled domestic scene. The top floor of Bushy House was adapted and used by the many children, who during the summer months could play outside in the park and lead a rural life. Although money was always short, there were continuous minor projects to enhance the inside and external aspects of the house, and the stables were reconstructed. William tried to resurrect his naval career to help with the Napoleonic War effort, but the Admiralty found means of thwarting what they regarded as an unwelcome contribution. However, he was able to lead the equivalent of the Home Guard in Teddington.

children of her previous relationships, she died in poor circumstances in France in 1816. By 18th-century standards the settlement would have appeared generous; by Victorian standards Mrs Jordan had no rights and should not be mentioned. In 21st-century eyes William's behaviour was appalling - dumping an older woman for more attractive younger ones, seeking to marry for money, and putting restrictions on the earnings of his ex-partner which did not exist when he was part beneficiary. The settlement can be seen as an exemplar of the inequity in rights between the sexes prevalent at the time.

William was not immediately successful in his pursuit of a wife. In his fifties, with boorish manners, he was not that attractive a proposition. The Prince Regent's only daughter died in childbirth in 1817, and pressure was put on William and his brothers

In 1811 William suddenly terminated the relationship with Mrs Jordan. His reasons were a mix of chasing a younger woman, pressing financial problems (his debts would not go away), and an aspiration to be free to marry a rich princess and acquire the financial security and respectability that would go with it. The settlement that was negotiated meant that Mrs Jordan left Bushy House, William had custody of their older children, and she received an income for herself and additional income for and custody of the younger children provided that she did not resume her career. In the event, she did return to the stage; later, dogged by ill health and financial problems associated with the

BUSHY HOUSE AND ITS GARDENS 2005
T19707k (Tom Holt)

to ensure the continuation of the Hanoverian line. William obtained a commitment to increased income from Parliament if he married (this was later reneged on), and after some failed attempts with other princesses, marriage with Princess Adelaide of Saxe Meiningen was agreed. Despite the age difference, the absence of any courtship, and the novelty of England for Adelaide, the marriage turned out well. The couple settled in Bushy House, and William continued his 'country squire' life. During this period there were major alterations made to Bushy House; these included a new look for the south facade looking out to Bushy Park, the enhancement of the servants' quarters, and the rearrangement of the stables. His attitude to Bushy Park was proprietorial - he farmed the area close to the house, and deforested much of the wider park. The public use of the

park was not welcome. William did visit the inns around the park, and attended some local functions; he was well regarded in the area. Adelaide brought a different set of attributes to Bushy House than her predecessor - she was a supporting, affectionate, and considerate companion to an older man, accepting ten stepchildren comfortably, and she had no career of her own.

The unexpected death of the Duke of York in 1827 with a childless marriage made William heir to the throne. At 6.30 in the morning on 26 June 1830 he was woken up in Bushy House to be told that George IV had died and he was now king. He took a fairly straightforward attitude to the ascension to the throne; he tried to keep the ceremonies simple, with the result that many saw it as a 'half coronation'. The family moved to London, with Windsor Castle the summer

residence; there were some celebrations and much goodwill from the local people on the couple's farewell to Bushy Park. William came to the throne at a very low ebb for the monarchy - George IV's attempts to 'divorce' Queen Caroline had been both unsuccessful and unpopular. At the age of 65, with a conservative outlook, William had to handle and accept the Reform Bill of 1832 and other contentious issues. He was not an unintelligent man, and the nickname 'Silly Billy' attached to him early in life (owing to his tendency to long, rambling and inconsequential speeches) was unfair. Against his instincts, he made the necessary compromises that led to the restriction on the monarch's involvement in politics and ability to appoint the prime minister. Neither he nor Adelaide were popular during the political struggles, as their conservative outlook was known. Nevertheless, by William's death in 1837, the monarchy had regained some credit before the reign of his successor Queen Victoria.

The Keepership of Bushy Park passed on to Queen Dowager Adelaide, and she returned to live in Bushy House. She was not well for much of her remaining twelve years, and never fully recovered from the early deaths of her children. She worshipped at St Mary's Church, and led a quiet life, giving to charity. One of her donations funded the first public boys' school in Teddington. She had developed good relationships with the family of the future Queen Victoria, and these were sustained after William's death. The general mourning on her death in 1849, led by Queen Victoria, was genuine. The memory of her runs wider than Teddington and its street and house names; the Australian city of Adelaide is named after her. Following her death, Bushy House was only intermittently used, apart from one long tenure by the Duc de Nemour, the second son of Louis Phillipe, who was involved in unsuccessful attempts to restore the French monarchy. The issue of occupancy was finally settled around the end of the century with the decision that it should be the home of the National Physical Laboratory, which opened there in 1902.

THE SIGN AT THE ADELAIDE, PARK ROAD 2005
T19708k (Tom Holt)

The first major economic change to life in Teddington in the 19th century occurred on the river. Before the coming of the railway and modern road traffic, rivers and canals were the primary route for transport of commercial goods. The town of Kingston, two miles upstream from Teddington, had become an inland port, thanks to the need to transport supplies to its breweries, distilleries, mills, tanneries and wharves. It also served as a staging point for transfer to road transport further inland. In his book 'The Thames from Hampton Court to Richmond', David McDowall provides a vivid picture of riverside life. Goods were carried by barges, which were designed for maximum efficiency. They were three to four feet in depth, long but narrow, and could carry 40 tons or up to 90 tons on the larger ones. In the 18th century the barges were pulled by gangs of men - a strenuous occupation, with good rewards, but serviced by the lower end of society, including convict gangs.

AN ENGRAVING OF THE FIRST TEDDINGTON LOCK ZZZ05473 (Richmond upon Thames Local Studies Collection)

THE BRIDGE 1899 43050

It would take over a week for goods to get from London Bridge to Kingston. By the 19th century the gangs had been replaced by horses; after disputes over rights of way with property owners and landowners, the towpaths that enabled horses to operate were established. Leading from London, these alternated between the Middlesex and Surrey sides: the towpaths transferred to the Surrey side at Twickenham, crossed to the Middlesex side at Kingston, and returned to the Surrey side at Hampton Court (this is the Thames Path route of today).

The regulation of the river by locks upstream and the impact of the London bridges reduced the water levels along this stretch of the river. The need to alter the currents to allow barges to avoid the shallows was recognised in a petition in 1775, and the bottlenecks, forcing queues of up to 20 barges, demanded action. After considering various plans the authorities agreed in 1810 to build five locks, the first of which was to be at Teddington. It was built of timber, and opened for traffic in 1811, with the weir following in 1812. The first lock keeper was Robert Savory, and the position remained in the Savory family for 50 years. It was not the most onerous position, although there were occasional attempts at robbing the takings. While a general success, the lock and weir did have some problems in the early years. These included damage from storms, the weir being broken by ice when the river froze in 1827, and opposition from some bargemasters over payment and prices.

By the 1840s the growing extraction of water in London and the resulting lower river levels forced a reconstruction of the lock. A new one designed for barges, with a side lock for leisure craft, was opened in

1858. The suspension bridge, designed on the style of Hammersmith Bridge, was put in place in 1889 at the cost of the Teddington community after continual attempts to get the Surrey side to pay ended in failure. There was heavy river traffic in the last part of the 19th century, which caused excessive queues. In response, the full double lock we are familiar with today was built and opened in 1904. By then, recreational traffic was taking a much greater share. It is the first lock on the river, it is where the tidal part of the Thames now ends, and it is the measuring point for the flow of water on the Thames.

If growth and ease of navigation was the dominant feature of the 19th century for river transport, the reverse was true for fishing. It was a story of depletion of stocks and restriction upon restriction on activity. A wide variety of fish are reported in the Thames at the start of the century, including salmon, trout, perch, flounder, carp, and a

FLOODS AT TEDDINGTON

One drawback of living in Teddington close to the river was occasional flooding. Horace Walpole mentions these at Strawberry Hill in 1756; the river level was at its highest for two centuries in 1774. A flood in 1852 lasted for weeks, with punts dealing with trade and people living upstairs. In 1877 the graveyard was again inundated, and the vicar of the day posted trespassing notices against those using the graveyard for boating amusement. In 1929, within the space of five months there was a severe summer drought exposing the river bed in the middle, followed by flooding in the autumn across the river banks and meadows. Sandbags were needed again in Manor Road and Ferry Road in 1975. The Thames Barrier was expected to mean the end of this, but Trowlock Island was still subject to flooding; upon enquiry, islanders were told that the barrier gates were only used when London itself was under threat.

THE BRIDGE 1899 43053

THE LOCK c1960 T19015

number of sea fish. But the environment had become hostile, with weirs, sewage and other pollution destroying habitats. By the middle of the century most of the fish species had disappeared or were in danger of doing so. Lamprey (an eel-like creature with a texture and flavour that was well regarded in Tudor and Stuart England, and still is in parts of southern Europe) were still breeding in fresh water and were fished in tons at Teddington in the 1850s, yet disappeared in the succeeding decades. Restrictions on fishing had started in the 17th century with regulations on weirs and nets. By the end of the 18th century these had been reinforced with £5 fines (a lot of money then) for fishing out of season, using certain types of nets, catching too young fish, and so on. The final step of banning netting of fish between Richmond and Staines was taken in 1860. That ended commercial fishing in Teddington. With considerable foresight,

a Thames Angling Preservation Society was formed in 1838. It was successful in sustaining angling, and was later able to start restocking the river. This stretch of the Thames once again became attractive for the sport.

By 1860 both Twickenham and Kingston were on the rail network. In 1863 the track through Teddington linking them was completed. Around the same time, the manor owners decided to sell their land. It was now possible to live in Teddington yet work in Kingston, Twickenham, Richmond or London itself, and land for housing was available. The outcome was swift, as the population figures show. In 1861 the village had 253 houses and a population of 1,183, about double the size it had been at the start of the century; by 1881 the population had reached 6,599, and in 1901 it was 14,037, occupying a few thousand houses. Teddington had transformed from village to suburb.

GARIBALDI VISITS TEDDINGTON

Victorian England was proud of its parliamentary system and constitutional monarchy. Leaders of European movements to overthrow autocratic monarchies were supported. Alexander Herzen, the Russian revolutionary and political author, had been exiled after periods of imprisonment by the tsar. He spent much of his time in England, and in 1863 and 1864 lived in Elmfield House, from where he continued to publish 'The Bell' and other inspiring literature and pamphlets aimed at ending serfdom, capital punishment, and the absolute monarchy of Tsarist Russia. One of the great romantic figures of the era was Garibaldi, who had led 'The Thousand' in liberating Sicily and then Naples from foreign rule, despite being heavily outnumbered. He then went on to liberate southern Italy in 1860. With the success of Cavour and the Piedmontese army in northern Italy, Italy had become close to unified and liberated, with only Venice and finally the end of papal rule in Rome to come in 1870. In 1864 Garibaldi visited London, where he was acclaimed by enthusiastic crowds estimated to number half a million. On 26 June he travelled to Teddington to meet Herzen. He was cheered all the way, with Teddington villagers shaking or kissing his hand as he arrived and celebrating his occasional appearances outside. The event also had some historical significance: Mazzini, the founder of Italian Unity movements and an exile since the 1830s, was present, and some reconciliation occurred between the two men, who had previously quarrelled and held different views of the future of the country they had so greatly helped to create.

ELMFIELD HOUSE, HIGH STREET 2005 T19709k (Tom Holt)

ORDNANCE SURVEY MAP OF TEDDINGTON 1912

The railway track was constructed along the most direct route, without great respect for the communities it cut through. In the case of Teddington the line eliminated the pond at the centre of the village and ran right across the common. It divided the village in two - literally so for a couple of years until the bridge was built at the foot of Waldegrave Road. To some extent this division persists today. Broad Street and the High Street have different characteristics, and there is no true centre of Teddington with all the main buildings concentrated together.

Before the arrival of the railways, Teddington had been a long village mainly strung along the High Street. The 1894 map shows a contrasting growth pattern. On the west side of the railway, Broad Street had been a country lane with a few houses, and there was open space beyond the public school situated on the corner of what is now Church Road. The main concentration of buildings had been along Park Road. By 1894 Broad Street had become the main street, with development running northwards along Stanley Road and Church Road to Shacklegate Lane and Fulwell and a number of fully built up streets running between them and to the west of Stanley Road. The area of Upper Teddington had been established, and was becoming heavily populated. By the end of the century, Broad Street and the Causeway

BROAD STREET c1895 ZZZ05474 (Richmond upon Thames Local Studies Collection)

ADVERTISEMENTS.

E. M. LEMON,
BAKER, CONFECTIONER,
Wine & Spirit Merchant,
HIGH STREET, TEDDINGTON.

Kinahan's L.L. Whiskey, 3/6 per bottle, Martell's and Hennessey's Champagnes, Sherries, Ports, &c.

Unrivalled Sponge & Pound Cakes.

HUNT & Co.,
WINE, SPIRIT,
and Bottled Beer Merchants.
London Gin, 2/-; Kinahan's Irish Whiskey, 3/6; The "Lorne" Scotch Whiskey, 3/6; Hennessy's and Martell's Brandy, 4/6; the celebrated "Red Heart" Rum, 3/6.

8, BROAD STREET, TEDDINGTON.

D. J. ROBERTS,
(PARISH SEXTON),
BRICKLAYER, PLASTERER,
SLATER & PAVER,
HIGH STREET, TEDDINGTON.

Estimates given for General Repairs.

Carpets Beaten, Drawn, and Swept by estimate or otherwise.

E. S. & M. LEMON,

BOOKSELLERS, PRINTERS

Stationers, &c.,

HIGH STREET

ADVERTISEMENTS IN TEDDINGTON PARISH MAGAZINE 1875 ZZZ05475
(Richmond upon Thames Local Studies Collection)

Lemon's on the High Street was still the main store in the 1870s; they sold groceries, bread, confectionery, drinks, and stationery, and also ran a library.

had become the 'modern' area, with the new shops, the post office, a bank, the Town Hall, the public school, and the cottage hospital. In contrast, the High Street retained some of its rural flavour and a mix of housing styles - many of the houses had front gardens on the High Street. Farms, market gardens and open land were still visible. Even up to 1908, Job's Dairy on the High Street used cows from fields at the back of the premises or adjacent to them. Towards the river, the large Victorian houses that run along the north side of the High Street and Ferry Road had appeared, but along the south side the old large houses still existed. The three-storey buildings that now characterise the south side of the High Street were built in a second surge of development at the end of the century and during the Edwardian period. Waldegrave Road was steadily being developed; the main industrial feature was still the wax bleaching and candle making factory (which was claimed to be among the largest in England). Large houses were built along the railway line on Fairfax Road, but the other side of the road still looked on to open space.

There were just a few large villas along the river in 1894. Around the turn of the century and (as the names of the roads indicate) during the Edwardian period, the streets between Broom Road and Kingston Road were built up down to Munster Road.

The novelist Richard Doddridge Blackmore was witness to this period of development. He had first come to the area in 1854, taking up a teaching post in Twickenham, and living in Hampton Wick. On the death of his father he inherited some money and bought land south of the High Street near the pond, where he built Gomer House. Apart from his professional writing work he developed a market garden, on which he made little profit over the years. He played chess at St Alban's Club on the High Street, but did not make a great impact on the community. He protested at the railway line running through his property and obtained some changes, but was unable to prevent the station being built opposite his house. He died childless, and eventually the property and Gomer House were sold. Some of the streets that emerged were named after him, Gomer House, and his most famous novel, 'Lorna Doone'.

The other major growth point was South Teddington. From virtually no population when the gasworks in Sandy Lane were built in 1851, there was rapid growth in the 1860s, mainly on the east side of the track. By the end of the century there was housing along Holmesdale Road, and streets of continuous housing stretched southwards from Bushy Park Road to Hampton Wick. The boundary between Teddington and Hampton Wick

DR LANGDON-DOWN ZZZ05521
(Courtesy of Langdon-Down Centre Trust)

became blurred, and from then on there has been much common community activity.

For 20th-century travellers along Kingston Road, the long Victorian building of Normansfield Hospital (recently partly demolished) had a sombre and rather forbidding presence. It had a remarkable history. Dr Langdon-Down was the son of an apothecary in Cornwall. After qualifying, he worked locally as a pharmacist with a period in London at the Pharmaceutical Society, where he helped Faraday on work investigating gases. He turned to medicine after the death of his father, proving to be a brilliant scholar. His first experience of mental health care came with his appointment in 1858 at the Earlswood Asylum for Idiots. It was here that he developed his belief that 'idiots' could have useful lives and a determination that they should be allowed them. During his years at Earlswood he set about putting his ideas into practice and also doing research. The most well known of his discoveries was the possibility of distinguishing between those illnesses with a genetic basis and those others where a person became mentally

ill during their lifetime. The condition of Down's Syndrome bears his name. He was not immune from the racial theories of his time, and the 'mongol' label was used by him for the condition (there is no physical justification for this).

In 1868 he raised loans and bought a plot of land between Teddington and Hampton Wick and constructed Normansfield Hospital, named after the solicitor who helped acquire the land.

Starting from an initial capacity to take on 19 patients, the site was developed and expanded to handle over 150 patients in the 1890s. The regime was supportive of the patients, with the accent on family-style care, without physical restraint or punishment. The facilities offered included a workshop, a men's club, and a laundry. Subsequently a farm was added (which reared animals commercially), a boathouse, and more workshops. The methods of care included what we would now call speech, occupational and play therapy. Dr Langdon-Down carried on with his Harley Street practice, and his wife, Mary, was the mainstay of the day-to-day management of the hospital. The Langdon-Down regime attracted international attention, and was regarded as among the most advanced in the field, with resulting visits from international groups of physicians.

Dr Langdon-Down died in 1896. His funeral was marked by the closing of shops, and many watched the cortege go through Kingston. His wife managed the hospital until her death in 1900, when responsibility passed to her sons.

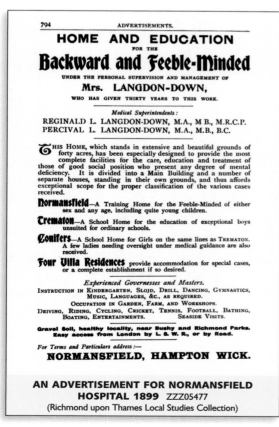

AN ADVERTISEMENT FOR NORMANSFIELD HOSPITAL 1899 ZZZ05477
(Richmond upon Thames Local Studies Collection)

THE THEATRE AT NORMANSFIELD HOSPITAL

An unusual feature of the Normansfield site was its theatre. Mr and Mrs Langdon-Down believed in entertainment as an enhancement to the lives of their patients, and put on simple plays and music for them in which some of the patients participated. The theatre opened in 1879. It had a full range of stage equipment, gas footlights, and a range of background scenery that could be swiftly interchanged. As well as entertaining the patients, the theatre was used for public performances. The Langdon-Downs founded the Genesta Amateur Dramatic Club in 1891, and there were public performances over the next eighteen years. Gilbert and Sullivan works were frequent, and Shakespeare and Oscar Wilde plays were also performed alongside more ephemeral works of the time. The club moved to the Surbiton Assembly Rooms in 1909.

NORMANSFIELD HOSPITAL THEATRE 2005
ZZZ05478 (Courtesy of Langdon-Down Centre Trust)

It became quickly clear that St Mary's Church was too small for the parish. In 1865 the Church of St Peter and St Paul on Broad Street was opened; it became independent of the parish in 1880. In South Teddington a mission church was formed in 1880, which later became St Mark's Church in the 20th century. When in 1884 the young Reverend Francis Boyd became the Vicar of Teddington, it was apparent that even with these changes the capacity of St Mary's Church would never cope with the new dimensions of the parish. He developed a vision for a church of cathedral proportions, and raised money for it. The new church, St Alban's, was built on the land opposite St Mary's Church. Its design followed that of a 13th-century church in France, and it was constructed in white stone rather than brick. The money ran out towards the end. The west end was boarded up, and the aisle was left with

five rather than the seven bays initially planned; the pulpit ended up more than half way down the church. Despite this reduction in size, the church building does have a cathedral scale, and was sometimes referred to as 'Thames Valley Cathedral'. It was and remains the largest indoor space in the borough. The green copper roof was visible from a distance, and in the 20th century it became a landmark for pilots landing at Heathrow.

ST ALBAN'S CHURCH 1899   43552

ST ALBAN'S CHURCH, THE INTERIOR 1899   43554

ST ALBAN'S CHURCH, THE INTERIOR 1899 43556

The services were 'High Church' in nature, and the ornamentation reflected that. Seven lamps were donated by the Orthodox Patriarch of Jerusalem after a visit there by Boyd; six of them were Russian, and one Venetian. St Alban's Church was consecrated in 1889 and again as the parish church in 1897 - St Mary's Church subsequently closed.

Francis Boyd was a magnetic speaker, and even the larger building could not contain the congregation on festival days. The St Alban's Day parades he instituted were grand occasions which stopped the traffic in the High Street. Kenneth Ingram, a local historian who witnessed many of them, wrote after Boyd's death: 'Those crowds! St Alban's remains particularly associated in my mind, perhaps, with crowds - crowds which thronged past the nave at Christmas Midnight Mass, which filled every corner of the church, even when St Alban's Day occurred in the middle of the week, and which stretched in a long queue round the stately grounds in which St Alban's stands, patiently waiting at Easter for an hour before the doors were opened'.

Alongside the expansion of the Church of England worship, a number of non-conformist communities appeared. By the end of the century a Methodist chapel was operating at the corner of Hampton Road and Stanley Road, and a Baptist community was well advanced, meeting in premises on Church Road where their church was eventually built. Christ Church on Station Road, which had started as a dissident parish offshoot protesting against what was seen as the semi-papist practice of the vicar in the 1860s, was now a flourishing independent free church. At the other end of the Christian spectrum, a Roman Catholic community grew in South Teddington, and the Church of Sacred Heart opened on Kingston Road in 1893.

If the churches did not have the capacity to deal with the living, they certainly could not cope with the dead. The council opened Teddington Cemetery in Shacklegate Lane in 1879, not without opposition from the churches, as the administration fell for the first time to a secular authority.

The development of education ran parallel to the churches in the 19th century. From the 1830s government funds were available to church schools, and the so-called National Schools were run by religious institutions. The school that Queen Adelaide had helped fund became Teddington Public School, sited near the Church of St Peter and St Paul on Broad Street, and girls' and infant classes were added to the boys' classes from the 1850s. A separate school was founded at Christ Church on Station Road for non-denominational education, and another school appeared on Old Schoolhouse Lane in South Teddington. A Catholic school on Fairfax Road near the church was opened in 1884.

The Education Act of 1870 made it compulsory to provide schools for children up to the age of ten, and compulsory attendance came in 1880. The borough decided against building what became known as Board Schools after the Act, and generally expanded the schools it already had. By

A CARD FOR TEDDINGTON PUBLIC SCHOOL
c1890 ZZZ05480
(Richmond upon Thames Local Studies Collection)

as a result of envy from others of his work, and later supervised the construction of a building in the Chilterns. He became heavily involved in the anti-Corn Law and Chartist activities in the 1840s. After arriving in London, he secured a post in the new Arts and Science Museum in South Kensington, and became responsible for promoting scientific education for boys and cookery education for girls. By the time he came to Teddington, in his late sixties, he was well known and also a JP. He became a councillor, and remained on the council with just one minor interruption

1899, 2,200 children attended schools in Teddington, of whom 800 were at Teddington Public School. The situation had transformed from the position early in the century when illiteracy was the norm. It is not surprising that education centred on the three Rs and preparation for labour or domestic life.

Education beyond school would have been exceptional at the time. One step was taken to further post-school learning and literacy. Books were expensive, and for some even borrowing from private libraries was beyond their means. The Public Library Acts were finally adopted by Teddington in 1895, but only on the basis of a couple of gas-lit rooms in a house on Broad Street with limited stock. One of the forceful Teddington figures of the time, John Charles Buckmaster, took up the issue. He had a background that reflected the century. Orphaned at the age of two in 1822, his early life was one of cruel beatings, hunger, and onerous work as a ploughboy. He took up carpentry, but had to move on

Fact File

The Collis Family

Today's Collis School is named after a member of a family that provided three long-serving contributors to Teddington community life. The original Collis couple arrived in Teddington in 1832. One of their daughters, Jane Collis, was postmistress at the post office on Broad Street for 27 years before her retirement in 1899. Sarah Collis set up a private school in 1865 and went on to be the founding headmistress of Christ Church School for 40 years. The school was named after her when it moved to Fairfax Road in 1972. Her niece May Collis was a teacher at the school from 1885 and took over as headmistress in 1906, finally retiring in 1928.

virtually till his death. A fierce advocate of technical and other education, he helped drive through a full implementation of a free library as a public service. The back garden of Elmfield House was chosen as the site, and money was obtained from Andrew Carnegie (a Scots-born American millionaire who funded libraries across the world). The Carnegie Library was opened in 1906 with a stock of over 1,000 books and a permanent librarian. Buckmaster's name on the foundation stones is a fitting memorial to him. A clock presented to him by the community in 1906 stands in the Reference Library.

Life in Teddington was not all work and no play. The river provided some recreation in the form of fishing, boating, and swimming. The common land that was left after the Enclosure Act of 1800 provided space for other outdoor activity, and so did Bushy Park. Club cricket was played on the common in the early 19th century, but the railway cut right through the ground when it was constructed. An imaginative appeal to the Crown was successful, and Bushy Park became home to Teddington Cricket Club and an emergent Hampton Wick Club. The first fixture at the ground in Bushy Park was between them in 1865. The two clubs prospered, and a pavilion was added to the facilities in 1893.

Provision for winter sports followed the summer ones. Teddington Hockey Club emerged from the cricket club. Its formation in 1871 occurred during a poor summer when cricketers were forced to other activity. This was the beginning of the formal game of hockey. The game spread to other clubs,

initially in Richmond and Surbiton, against whom the first competitive games were played. These were not frequent, as transport was still by horse-drawn carriages at the time. The minutes of the meeting of the Hockey Club in April 1875 record a 'letter from the Hon Secretary of Richmond Hockey Club proposing a Hockey Conference' to set out the rules of the game. This was much needed, as the same minutes record concern at the practice of 'hitting which appears to lie greatly on the increase. It is contrary to the Rules of the Game and lessens the enjoyment of the players'. The conference did occur, but it took until the late 1880s

Public Announcements.

FOOTBALL AND HOCKEY.

A GRAND MATCH will be played in the

OLD DEER PARK,

On SATURDAY, NOVEMBER 7TH, 1874,

Between the RICHMOND CLUB and the ROYAL MILITARY ACADEMY (WOOLWICH), commencing at half-past Three.

On the same day and place, will also be played a second football match between RICHMOND and the CRANBROOK ROVERS, and a

HOCKEY MATCH

between RICHMOND and TEDDINGTON.

On THIS occasion the following charges for admission to the ground will be made:—

Persons on foot .... 0s 6d.
Persons on horseback .... 1s 0d.
Carriages .... 2s 6d.

AN ANNOUNCEMENT OF A HOCKEY MATCH IN 1874 ZZZ05481 (Teddington Hockey Club)

before the rules were agreed and codified. The Teddington strip of chocolate and pink shirts with dark blue trousers (not shorts!) first appeared in 1886.

School and summer trips from London to Hampton Court and Bushy Park had started after Queen Victoria opened them to the public early in her reign. Visitor numbers grew extensively after Hampton Court and Teddington stations were opened. The spring blossoms of the chestnut trees became an attraction, and Chestnut Sunday processions developed; they were in full flow at the end of the century and in the Edwardian period, even attracting the presence of royalty.

THE THAMES c1955 T19006

A CHESTNUT SUNDAY POSTCARD c1910 ZZZ05525 (Bushy Park Archives)

In 1874, when cycling was still a novelty, an invitation to meet in Bushy Park attracted a significant response. By their peak in 1882 the great bicycle meets with early pennyfarthing bicycles and tricycles attracted over 2,000 participants, and had become grand occasions with large crowds observing the events. The rapid general expansion of cycling, after more robust penny farthing bicycles emerged, brought the Bushy Park meets to an end by the end of the decade as more local events were arranged and clubs appeared across London.

Summer Sundays at Teddington Lock were also busy, with people arriving to watch or use leisure craft, to swim or fish, and to take refreshments in the Angler's pub by the footbridge.

THE ANGLER'S HOTEL AND THE RIVER 1890 23538

A PENNY FARTHING BICYCLE MEET AT BUSHY PARK c1880 ZZZ05482 (Richmond upon Thames Local Studies Collection)

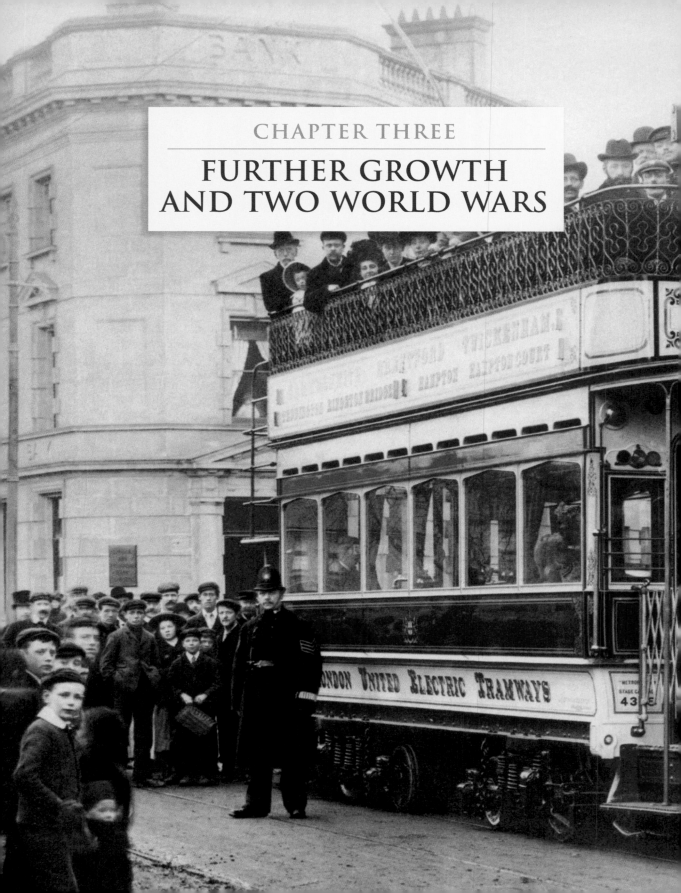

CHAPTER THREE

FURTHER GROWTH
AND TWO WORLD WARS

IF a current resident of Teddington took a walk through Edwardian Teddington, they would find much that is familiar - the layout of the roads, the basic architecture of the High Street and some of Broad Street, whole and part streets of terraced and semi-detached housing, and the location of the churches and some of their buildings. In contrast the shops and their contents would look different, the variety of food on offer in the cafes and restaurants would feel very limited, the schools would be unfamiliar, and the hospital would not be in the same place. The absence of cars and aircraft noise would be another noticeable difference. Many of the changes occurred after the Second World War, but several took place before it.

Electricity had already come to Teddington by the beginning of the 20th century. As a consequence, there was a major change in road public transport. Horse-drawn carriages and omnibuses had been the main vehicles in the late 19th century. Their replacement by electric trams was not uncontroversial - apart from general resistance to change and the vested interest of the previous providers of transport, there was the inconvenience and expense of widening roads, the noise, and the need to give way to trams on the road. On the other hand, there were those who saw the advantage of speed, the likely commercial benefits for shops, and a long-overdue upgrade of the roads that horse-drawn traffic deteriorated and dirtied. Teddington became one of the battlegrounds for London United Tramways, with the council opposed to them. The energy and political manoeuvering that accompanied the debate far exceeded any interest in national issues. After the success of their allies in the local elections, and an offer to pay for road widening and bridge strengthening, London United Tramways won the battle and the tracks were laid. The first tram journey through Teddington took place on 2 April 1903 amid much ceremony. The event achieved national attention, with the Daily Telegraph reporting: 'There are those that think the very sleepiness of Teddington and Hampton Wick is part of their charm. So it is, but nobody cares to eternalise narrow and impassable lanes, and in broadening and straightening the roading the company have done a permanent service ... To be gifted by Nature and not allowed to enjoy Nature's gifts is a crabbed condition from which the electric fairy is going, in part at least, to save us.' The early tram route was similar to the current 281 bus route, running from Fulwell along Stanley Road, Broad Street, the High Street, and turning right down Kingston Road to Hampton Wick. Here it turned right to Hampton Court rather than across Kingston Bridge (which needed widening before trams could use it); it then completed a loop back to Fulwell via Hampton and Hampton Hill. In practice the benefits of trams were soon evident, even if the price paid was the truncation or elimination of attractive front gardens on the High Street.

Later in the century the trams, whose speeds did not exceed ten miles per hour, were replaced by trolley buses that were quieter and could run at double the speed. The inaugural trolley bus journey in 1931

A FIRST-DAY TRAM ON BROAD STREET 2 APRIL 1903 ZZZ05516 (Graham Sims Collection)

was also the first one in London, and hence an occasion was made of it with the Lord Mayor, aldermen and councillors on board a decorated bus. The early trolley bus journeys were not always smooth - drivers still had to learn to handle the new vehicles. One witness recalls seeing one crash across the fence and into the grounds of St Alban's Church. The final trolley bus journey on 8 May 1962, before diesel buses fully took over, was also the last ever London trolley bus journey. It was witnessed by thousands as it took the route from Wimbledon via New Malden, Kingston, and Teddington, arriving at Fulwell just before midnight. During the day a ceremonial trip was run with one of the

early 'Diddler' trolley buses taking the original route to Teddington; pupils at St Peter's and St Mary's School joined the crowds along Broad Street that watched it go by. The depot at Fulwell was the centre of operations in the area for London United Tramways, and is now the current bus station.

The shopkeepers were justified in supporting the tramways. With Broad Street and the High Street linked and easily accessible, the next 50 years were the heyday for independent shopkeepers and local chains. Deayton's Stores on Broad Street (ZZZ05516, above) had opened in the 1880s with the novelty of offering on one site groceries, fruit and vegetables, bread, meat, basic hardware, china, glass and other goods - in effect a mini department store. Other more specialist shops followed along the Causeway and Broad Street, among them florists, fishmongers, butchers, bakers, dairies, stationers, printers, confectioners, tailors, hairdressers, cleaners, tobacconists, a furniture store, and (important in the 1930s) a pawnbroker's. Some of the shops were built into the front gardens of Victorian terraces (one shopkeeper explored underneath and found evidence of the old boilers and kitchens). This side of Teddington became a typical busy suburban shopping precinct. The shops stretched into Stanley Road, and on Fridays and Saturdays barrows appeared in Elleray Road, staying ready for business until well into the evening. Sunday was a day of rest, observed with shops closed and pub hours restricted.

In the eyes of someone crossing over the railway bridge, the High Street scene was different and more like a country town. The architecture was less uniform, the shops were more spread out, more were built on the front gardens of old houses, and there were more establishments providing professional services. Some of the shops had an up-market flavour; these traders were still seeing their role as supplying the 'big houses', taking orders and despatching the purchases directly to them. Lemon's on the south side ran a business that provided cakes, confectionery, pastries and catering for weddings and special occasions. It had started well back in the 19th century. Tozer's (another baker's) had also been there in the 19th century, as had Poupart's and Job's dairies (whose origins dated back to 1819). Dowsett's provided a travel agent

SCOTT'S, THE BUTCHERS ON BROAD STREET c1910 ZZZ05483 (Richmond Local Studies Collection)

HIGH STREET c1910 ZZZ05484 (Richmond Local Studies Collection)

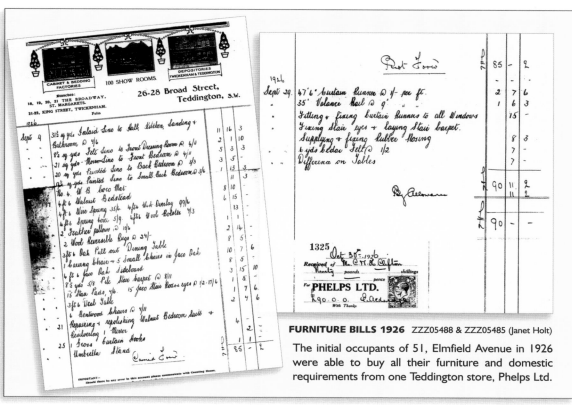

FURNITURE BILLS 1926 ZZZ05488 & ZZZ05485 (Janet Holt)

The initial occupants of 51, Elmfield Avenue in 1926 were able to buy all their furniture and domestic requirements from one Teddington store, Phelps Ltd.

A FAMILY BUSINESS

SIMS THE OPTICIAN'S, DECORATED FOR THE CORONATION 1953 ZZZ05520 (Graham Sims Collection)

Very few Teddington establishments have lasted the century. One family business that has is Sims on the Causeway. In 1902, after a period as an apprentice, Albert George Sims, who hailed from Shaftesbury, opened a watchmaking and jewellery store; optical work was a sideline, covering pince-nez and other decorative aids to sight. He ran the store until 1936. His son of the same name developed the optical side from 1922 and converted the enterprise into an optician's when his father retired. His wife ran it after he died in 1950. In turn their two sons also went into optical work. The elder, Ian, became a clinician. The younger, Graham, took to the dispensing side and is the current proprietor; his daughter has been a partner since 1992. He has witnessed the change from standard NHS provision of plastic spectacles with months of waiting to today's varifocal and other lenses, a wide range of designer frames, swift supply, and direct payment by the customer.

service, and Pomfrett's special transport, with carriages for important occasions. There was an antique store, and a music shop with sheet music for the popular songs of the day and 78rpm gramophone records.

The 1921 census showed a population increase of 50% for Teddington since 1901. Within this statistic there was a grim subtext: there were 20% more women then men in the 20-34 age group. The primary cause of this disparity between males and females was the carnage of the First World War.

There may have been little damage to the fabric of Teddington during the conflict of 1914-18, but more British lives were lost than in the Second World War. The experience in Teddington was not that different from elsewhere - the pressure to volunteer, conscription, rationing, the regular receipt of news of deaths of loved ones, the return of the injured, and finally peace on Armistice Day and the arrival back of surviving soldiers. There was some specific war effort in Teddington. Part of Bushy Park was converted into allotments to increase food supply. Also, the National Physical Laboratory programmes were expanded to include support to the production of shells and fuses, air navigation research, and, on a more sombre note, the calibration of clinical thermometers to be used in the care of the wounded. Women took over occupations previously the preserve of men, and some of this became permanent - the 1921 Census for Teddington showed the same female percentage participation in the workforce as before, but the jobs were now secretarial or in shops rather than domestic service, even if these new jobs were still subordinate in nature.

A war memorial in Portland stone with 337 names was erected and dedicated in 1921. Its location in front of Teddington's hospital is not a coincidence, for the whole hospital was conceived as a memorial to the war dead. The story, set out in L Arthur Wyatt's book on Teddington's hospitals, starts in 1874 when Thomas Chappell, head of a piano maker's and music publisher's in London, chaired a meeting in his home

THE CANADIAN CONVALESCENT HOSPITAL AT UPPER LODGE, BUSHY PARK c1915 ZZZ05528 (© The Royal Parks)

Canadian troops were camped in Bushy Park during the war, and Upper Lodge was used as a convalescent hospital and home for their wounded. After the war King George V gave permission for Upper Lodge to be used as a holiday home for poor East End children.

to discuss setting up a cottage hospital for the sick poor of Teddington. A public meeting followed to discuss the fact that, despite the increased population, 'no hospital accommodation for the inhabitants of these parishes (Teddington and Hampton Wick) exists nearer than Richmond Infirmary on the one side ... and Kingston Union on the other'; the meeting agreed the desirability of establishing a cottage hospital. Events progressed rapidly after that. Early in 1875 the Teddington and Hampton Wick Cottage Hospital opened in two semi-detached houses in Elfin Grove north of Broad Street, using their rear gardens to extend into. A dispensary was added in 1882, and the hospital expanded to ten beds in 1892.

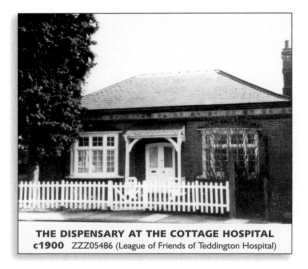

THE DISPENSARY AT THE COTTAGE HOSPITAL c1900 ZZZ05486 (League of Friends of Teddington Hospital)

This was long before the NHS and social insurance; the target was to provide for those who were too poor to pay for their treatment, but who were above the poverty line for Kingston Workhouse Infirmary. 74% of the hospital's income came from subscriptions, donations, gifts (within which Thomas Chappell's own contribution was significant), and fund-raising events. One crisis was met by the 'Shilling Fund', organised by the Surrey Comet, to which over 5,000 Teddington residents and other individuals subscribed.

The cottage hospital came into operation at a time when Teddington's population was just over 4,000. It could not cater for the fivefold population increase that followed, let alone the consequences of the First World War. A new hospital was needed. David Anderson, whose family had run a nursery garden on Hampton Road, offered this as a site, and the land was acquired on a lease-back arrangement to signal the intent. The new hospital project became the focus of Teddington charitable

OUR GLORIOUS DEAD

1914

THE FIRST WORLD WAR MEMORIAL, HAMPTON ROAD 2005 T19710k (Vicky Higgin)

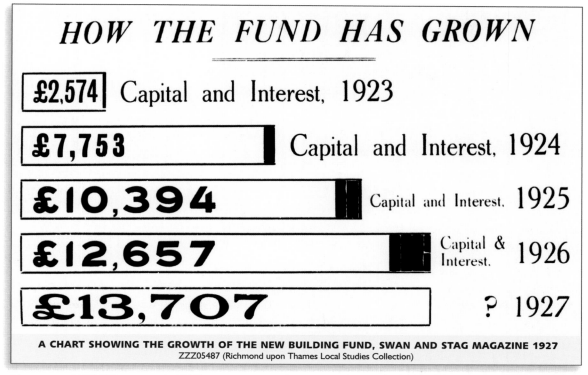

HOW THE FUND HAS GROWN

£2,574	Capital and Interest, 1923
£7,753	Capital and Interest, 1924
£10,394	Capital and Interest. 1925
£12,657	Capital & Interest. 1926
£13,707	? 1927

A CHART SHOWING THE GROWTH OF THE NEW BUILDING FUND, SWAN AND STAG MAGAZINE 1927
ZZZ05487 (Richmond upon Thames Local Studies Collection)

The target of £18,000 was met in 1927; an impressive achievement when multiplied by 30 to get to today's prices and occuring at time when there was little disposable income after the cost of rent, food and basic clothing.

fundraising for the next decade. There were annual carnivals and fetes, funding a brick schemes, and individual events often run by local sports and other clubs. It still took until 1927 to raise the money to be able to contract for the construction of the hospital on a 'no profit' basis. Teddington Memorial Hospital opened in 1929 after a protracted period of building and some financial crises - the eventual opening date was dictated by the collapse of the water cistern in the old hospital. The new hospital was not just a replacement for the cottage hospital. It was on a larger scale, with two wards of twelve beds, X-ray equipment, and an operating theatre, and an adequate dispensary. There were also proper administrative support and domestic facilities for staff. Hugh Munby, the driving force and Chair of the Management Committee, lived to see the opening, but died suddenly a few months afterwards. In a second phase of construction, a children's ward and further beds were added, raising the capacity to 46 beds. This was now a hospital for the community, not only the poor, and the economics reflected that. At the time of the hospital's absorption into the NHS in 1947, the source of its income had reversed, with nearly 70% coming from patients rather than charitable sources and investment income.

NOEL COWARD

'I cannot remember
I cannot remember
The house where I was born,
But I know it was in Waldegrave Road,
Teddington, Middlesex,
Not far from the borders of Surrey,
An unpretentious abode
Which, I believe, economy forced us to leave
In rather a hurry.'

Thus did Noel Coward recall his early childhood at 131 Waldegrave Road, where Teddington's only blue plaque was unveiled in 1995 by Donald Sinden. Coward's mother had moved to Teddington in 1883, and met his father at choir practice in St Alban's Church. The family was very active in the church, and contributed greatly to its musical life. They left Teddington abruptly, and were living in Sutton in 1905. In a writing career that spanned 60 years and earned him a knighthood, Noel Coward wrote plays, songs, and a novel, and scripted many films. Among his works are 'Blithe Spirit', 'London Pride', 'In Which We Serve', and 'Brief Encounter'. Although his later life was far removed from his origins, he reflected warmly on his South London suburban origins in his autobiography.

THE NOEL COWARD BLUE PLAQUE
1995 ZZZ05489 (Graham Watson)

Another insight from the 1921 Census was the employment pattern. For every Teddington resident employed within the borough, there was one working in London and another working in one of the neighbouring boroughs of Richmond, Twickenham or Kingston. Commuting had become the Teddington norm. The reason for Teddington's being a net exporter of labour was that there were no really large commercial employers. The arrival of electricity drastically reduced the demand for the products of the wax and candle making factory on Waldegrave Road; this closed, and the premises were converted to house the Paint Research Association in 1927. On the river there had been a boat repair facility since the 1850s; at the turn of the century it was in the hands of Henderson & Tough, whose main facilities were in Blackfriars. Douglas Tough, from a junior branch of the family, set up a separate business that in the inter-war years offered boat repairs, passenger services, and yacht and dinghy repairs. In 1938 he acquired the neighbouring premises and was in a position to expand.

The largest employer in Teddington became the NPL (National Physical Laboratory). The origins of the NPL arose from concerns over the weakening British industrial position in competition with the USA and Germany, where the national investment in science was higher and its deployment in industry and commerce was more pervasive. When the Prince of Wales opened the laboratory in 1902 he indicated that 'the objective of the scheme is to bring scientific knowledge to bear practically upon everyday commercial and industrial life'. He missed the military dimension. The establishment of the NPL grew from an initial nineteen staff to just under 200 at the outset of the First World War. It was then discovered that not only was Britain behind Germany on many key fronts, but also dependent on it for whole areas of technology. A vital one was optical glass, where there was a military need for telescopes, binoculars, compasses, rangefinders, and periscopes. There was a similar need in the

production of munitions. The NPL became part of the operation to equip Britain in these fields. The workforce doubled during the war in response - it was mostly made up of women. At the end of the war returning men took back many of the posts, but the NPL still employed a significant number of women and retained its innovative equal pay regime.

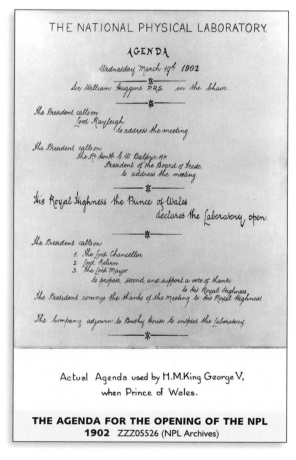

THE NATIONAL PHYSICAL LABORATORY.

AGENDA

Wednesday March 19th 1902

Sir William Huggins P.R.S. in the chair

The President calls on
Lord Rayleigh
to address the meeting.

The President calls on
The Rt. Hon'ble A.W. Balfour M.P.
President of the Board of Trade
to address the meeting.

His Royal Highness the Prince of Wales
declares the Laboratory open.

The President calls on
1. The Lord Chancellor
2. Lord Kelvin
3. The Lord Mayor
to propose, second, and support a vote of thanks
to His Royal Highness.
The President conveys the thanks of the meeting to His Royal Highness.

The Company adjourn to Bushy House to inspect the Laboratory.

Actual Agenda used by H.M.King George V, when Prince of Wales.

**THE AGENDA FOR THE OPENING OF THE NPL
1902** ZZZ05526 (NPL Archives)

The work of the inter-war years had less urgency. Contrary to the traditional British image of scientific research - other-worldly white-coated men playing with complicated apparatus and communicating in incomprehensible algebra - the work of the NPL has always had a firm practical foundation and many wide-reaching practical outcomes. In a society increasingly dependent on technology, the importance of standards and the national use of it could not be underestimated. It really did start to matter that what one scientist or manufacturer called 200 degrees Celsius was the same as what another called 200 degrees Celsius, and that measuring gauges worked accurately. As electricity became widespread, it was necessary to have proper measurement of flow, power, and resistance, and reliable instruments for calibration. Similarly, as electric lighting became the norm, calibration was needed on luminosity strength for use in homes, shops, and museums and galleries, and for signalling in road, rail and air transport. Other tasks of measurement were required by the technologies that emerged in the inter-war years - X-rays for medical and industrial purposes, refrigeration materials and their impact on food, fatigue of new materials under high levels of stress, and the commercial and military use of wireless technology as the radio and gramophone industries developed. The new aeronautical industry also needed support in the design and control of aircraft, and wind tunnels were erected on site to enable the necessary experiments and measurement to take place.

By the 1930s the programmes of the NPL had crystallized into four main streams - assistance to industry on immediate problems, research on longer term possibilities for industry, the testing of instruments, and

maintenance of the standards on which all physical measurement is based (in collaboration with other nations). This involved expansion, and more of Bushy Park and neighbouring streets were taken into the NPL. As the international climate grew more difficult with the emergence of Nazi Germany, Britain was far better placed in terms of national scientific support for the struggle to come than it had been at the outset of the First World War.

A quite different enterprise grew on Broom Road. In the 1880s Weir House on the river was owned by Henry Chinnery, a wealthy stockbroker, who was interested in cinema. He allowed some local enthusiasts to use his greenhouse for filming. This grew, with Ek-co Films shooting silent comedies from 1912. In the 1920s the facilities expanded to take over the house. By the time the giant American film company Warner Brothers took over in 1931, there were two 75ft x 55ft studios, water tanks for sea films, and large gardens available as scenery reaching down to a 150-yard river frontage. A very efficient production line was established by Warner Brothers, with the studios churning out over 100 films over the next eight years. They were aimed at the British audience, and were generally 'B' feature films with plots such as 'a cockney girl unmasks crooks posing as ghosts', 'a novelist imagines a murder involving his fellow boarders', 'gang seeks jewels already stolen by rivals', 'charlady on prize holiday saves baby prince from revolutionaries'. Some famous names appeared in them - Rex Harrison, Margaret Lockwood, Charles Hawtry, Joan

Hickson (later the TV Miss Marple) and Jack Hawkins. Max Miller featured in seven comedies filmed here, and Errol Flynn began his career in one of the films and was promptly whisked off to Hollywood once his talent was recognized.

Houses were built on most of the remaining available land - this was mainly between Park Road and Sandy Lane; to the north and south of the High Street; and along Fairfax Road. Fulwell and the streets west of Stanley Road became fully established, with a new school, the bus depot, and the construction of St James's Church. A shopping parade developed on Stanley Road at the Shacklegate Lane junction. Palmers, the cycle shop, has been there from the start over a century ago.

Fact File

When the Grove House estate came on the market in 1920, the Royal Dutch Shell Company bought it and created a Dutch-style environment with open gardens and specifically designed centrally heated houses for its employees to live in. At the centre there were open areas, which are now Grove Gardens. Some people have recalled a special tunnel under Twickenham Road leading to the Lensbury boathouse on the river, but no survey has actually confirmed its existence.

HOUSES IN THE GROVE 2005 T19711k (Vicky Higgin)

HOUSES FOR BOATING MEN.
Broom Water, Teddington.
FRONTING SAILING REACH AND ABOVE LOCK.

A BOON TO BOATING MEN.— The water needs of the large class of owners of sailing and rowing boats who cannot afford the usually costly riverside cottage, or "mansion and grounds," are especially to be regarded. A building estate has just been opened, where these points are to be kept in view by the construction of a canal giving each house direct access to the river as well as room for mooring, &c., along its own frontage.—*Westminster Gazette.*

Fifteen Minutes from Teddington and Hampton Wick Stations, and within easy reach of Hampton Court and Richmond Park.

VIEW FROM BROOM ROAD.
GROUND LEVEL WELL ABOVE HIGHEST FLOODS.

Gas ; Water ; Main Drainage ; Electric Bells ; Tiled Stoves and Hearths ; Hot and Cold Water ; Perfect Sanitation ; and Balcony and Verandah overlooking Water.

It has often been found that boating men with moderate means find difficulty in getting, at reasonable cost, a house where launches or boats can be kept moored at the bottom of the garden ready for amateur repairs or immediate use. To meet the requirements of this class a new estate for residential property has been opened up a little way above the lock at Teddington. This novel idea of making what is practically a new river was carried out by digging trenches along the sides, and constructing battered cement concrete retaining walls from one foot below the bottom to the water level, and then digging out the centre. The spoil was used to raise the general level of the property. During the progress of the works the land water was kept down by powerful steam centrifugal pumps, and so excellent was the gravel that the concrete walls made with it did not show one single crack throughout the entire length.—*The British Architect.*

'HOUSES FOR BOATING MEN' ADVERTISEMENT c1900 ZZZ05522 (Broom Water Association)

An unusual development had occurred at Broom Water. A small creek had been extended by a property developer by 1894, and in the succeeding years he built 21 houses on Broom Water and up to No 12 Broom Water West before going bankrupt in 1907. They were advertised as 'Houses for Boating Men' and there was a boathouse at the back of one of them. Nos 14 and 16 were added by 1915, and the remainder of the houses on the two streets were built between 1930 and 1965. The creek is, in effect, a private waterway. There have been regattas since 1906 for many types of boats and for all ages. This is now a conservation area, and the Broom Water Association takes care of the environment as well as running social events.

Teddington residents tended to go elsewhere for their organised entertainment, particularly after the town hall, which had a dance hall and theatre, was burnt down in 1903. St Mary's Church had already hosted concerts in the 1880s (with the Coward quartet an attraction), and the new St Alban's Church hosted organ recitals and choir concerts during the Edwardian period, including an early performance of Elgar's 'The Dream of Gerontius'. These petered out after the First World War. Teddington Theatre Club was formed in 1927 by a group of teachers to perform Shakespeare and other plays, and proved more durable. It reached acknowledged high standards of production; after a peripatetic existence, with bases including Elleray Hall and Ronayne Hall and venues in Twickenham, it secured a permanent home in Hampton Court House in 1971 (with a later move to a new theatre in Hampton Hill in 1999 made possible by Lottery Funding). The number of performances steadily grew from four one-night productions per annum to four-night productions ten or more times per annum. The repertoire is wide-ranging, from Ibsen to light comedies and musicals.

THE CREEK AT BROOM WATER c2000 ZZZ05490
(Broom Water Association)

It is hard to believe that this scene is in a built up area like Teddington. The children are participating in one of the regattas.

Sporting institutions grew in this period. The Teddington Tennis Club on Vicarage Road started, along with Teddington Bowls Club (playing at a green by the Clarence Hotel near the station, and not at today's green in Grove Gardens), and the Fulwell golf course was laid out. After a long campaign for an open-air swimming pool, one was constructed and opened in 1931 in Vicarage Road. Pictures of Teddington Lido look very old-fashioned, but the welcome for the facility was remarkable, with high attendances in the summer months. Teddington Swimming Club started within the year.

- St HeLENS Court and FinsBURY Circus. A third house and extra land was taken in 1921, and the club was later linked with BP's equivalent. All forms of sports took place, and there was a lively drama and entertainment group as well as indoor billiards, bridge and chess clubs. In 1936 the house and grounds next door became available at a low price when the bank that owned them went bankrupt. These were acquired and the old buildings demolished. The construction of the modern Lensbury building was completed in 1938, with a cricket ground looking onto the river and tennis courts.

A SKETCH FROM THE OPENING PROGRAMME OF TEDDINGTON SWIMMING BATHS 1931
ZZZ05491 (Richmond upon Thames Local Studies Collection)

Private sports grounds were created for institutions and colleges. The largest was for the Lensbury Club. The Royal Shell Company was in need of temporary accommodation for some of its employees and visitors, and in 1920 took over two houses on Broom Road and the land opposite and formed the Lensbury Club. The name was a composite from the locations of the two London offices at the time

On the river two significant sporting clubs appeared. The origin of the Royal Canoe Club was a meeting in 1865 at the Star and Garter Hotel, which set it up; in the following year the first regatta and races took place. The first long-distance race between Teddington Lock and Putney Bridge followed. The 'Royal' status came in 1873. The club moved from Kingston to Trowlock Island in 1897.

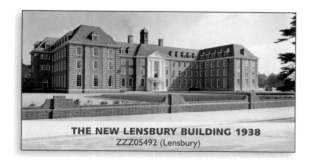

THE NEW LENSBURY BUILDING 1938
ZZZ05492 (Lensbury)

The Royal Canoe Club represented the country in the 1936 Berlin Olympics and subsequent Olympics. The Tamesis Club was formed in 1885 and joined with four other clubs in 1888 to form the Sailing Club Association. When their clubhouse at Hampton Wick burnt down in 1901, they moved to Trowlock. By then the annual pattern of river sailing had been set, with an Easter regatta at Teddington, followed by ones at other locations on the Thames and at sea in the summer months, returning to

ELMFIELD HOUSE DECORATED FOR THE SILVER JUBILEE OF KING GEORGE V 1935
ZZZ05493 (Richmond upon Thames Local Studies Collection)

Teddington for an autumn regatta.

The 1935 Silver Jubilee celebrations for King George V involved decorations on the main buildings and shops. During the day there was a united service from the churches in Bushy Park. In the evening St Alban's and St Mary's Church were floodlit. There was a torchlight procession in Bushy Park, and a fireworks display in the garden of Bushy House.

National political events and movements rarely made a great impact on Teddington. The Suffragette Movement and the 1926 National Strike barely registered, and the Great Depression of the 1930s was less severe here than elsewhere. In contrast, when Britain was facing the prospect of foreign domination and imposition of an alien regime contrary to its democratic traditions, the Teddington population and those who worked in the area made notable contributions, initially to Britain's lone resistance in Western Europe and later to the Allied victory over Nazi Germany and its allies.

Teddington's institutions were already being put on a war footing in the late 1930s. The NPL's programme was enhanced and directed towards military objectives; the hospital geared up to dealing with expected civilian casualties; and expanded boat building capacity became available. Yet the first major contribution turned out to be a reactive one. The swift German advance on Belgium and northern France in May 1940 was so successful that the British Expeditionary Force was suddenly left isolated in Dunkirk. The waters were too shallow for the normal navy ships to save the 340,000 soldiers stranded there.

Douglas Tough, among others, received a call from the Ministry of Shipping asking him to act as an agent to secure small craft for an expedition from Ramsgate and Sheerness to rescue the soldiers. He commandeered over 100 boats, some willingly brought by owners, others taken without their knowledge. The boats were fuelled, oiled and made fit for the voyage and then were crewed by volunteers from Teddington to Sheerness. It is estimated that 5,000 soldiers were saved by these particular vessels as the British force was evacuated and saved. Tough then had the task of returning the vessels to their owners (not all of whom were happy at their indirect contribution to this heroic war episode).

By 1941 most of the NPL's work was

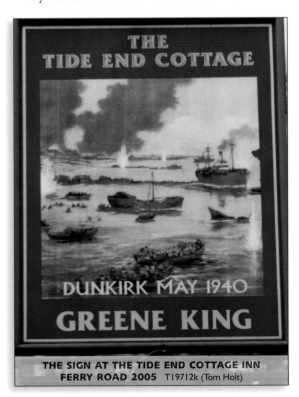

**THE SIGN AT THE TIDE END COTTAGE INN
FERRY ROAD 2005** T1971 2k (Tom Holt)

dedicated to war ends. The NPL made important contributions to improvements in war aircraft and their navigation, to advances in wireless communication, and to the strengthening of metal plates and cylinders against shell and other weaponry. Its maritime work was heavily involved in the security of transport against mines and torpedoes, confining fire damage, designing more robust lifeboats, enhancing aircraft carriers and their operation, and the design of the pontoons to be used in the invasion of Normandy. The most renowned product of the laboratory in the war was the 'bouncing bomb', developed under Barnes Wallis, which was used in the later bombing of German industrial and military capacity, and was famously portrayed in the film 'The Dam Busters'.

Tough's boatyard went into production of the Fairmile Craft, which were used to lay mines, escort convoys, and assist in sea/air rescue work. By 1944 some 200 staff were being deployed in this work, and in repair operations locally and along the Thames. Warner Brothers' film production was reduced, and some of it was directed at morale-raising films before a bomb in 1944 destroyed the studios and killed the director, 'Doc' Salomon.

Unlike the situation in the First World War, the civilian population was under threat; Teddington was a target for aerial bombardment owing to the presence of its NPL and the riverside production activity. The Teddington Society produced a community play, 'Careless Talk', to commemorate the 50th anniversary of the war-time effort.

Fact File

Teddington had its own cinema. The Savoy was situated next to Elmfield House on the High Street opposite the post office, and opened at the beginning of the century. Its audiences grew, and it had to be rebuilt in 1937. During the war it was particularly popular, as entertainment was scarce; occasionally excitement in the films was interrupted by the real-life drama of evacuation during air raids. Audiences declined in the 1950s, and the cinema closed in 1960.

SAVOY CINEMA, HIGH STREET c1950 ZZZ05494 (Richmond upon Thames Local Studies Collection)

As part of the project they conducted a wide survey of personal reminiscences, which are available in Teddington Library. These speak for themselves, and vividly cover the local experience of the main events of the war. On the phoney war and its false alarms and minor raids, one memory ran: 'Much of the time spent in the shelters where a lot of knitting for the forces was achieved'. Then the Blitz: 'Who could forget that terrible night of 29 November 1940. The constant screaming of bombs and loud blasts that rocked the ground ... my father became a hero in the eyes of neighbours for putting out an incendiary bomb that had set fire to their roof ... I recall the horror of seeing the ghastly devastation all round the following morning and particularly the burnt out shell of our lovely church - the Baptist in Church Road'. Later in the war: 'Doodlebugs were really scary ... the warning

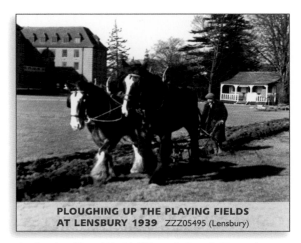

PLOUGHING UP THE PLAYING FIELDS AT LENSBURY 1939 ZZZ05495 (Lensbury)

As in the First World War, playing fields and parts of Bushy Park were used to grow food.

signal would go tweet and you knew one was approaching your area, then came the sounds of the engine and you would hold your breath whilst it droned on and heaved a sigh of relief when it had passed over ... if you heard the engine cut out you knew that within a few minutes you would either be dead or alive'. On rationing: 'As a housewife it was very difficult. We had to queue for everything and I never knew what there was to eat ... the clinic was excellent and provided orange juice, cod liver oil and powdered milk for my baby'. The American camp in Bushy Park: 'Many Americans were billeted in the park and our lovely park was cut up and built upon. Officers were billeted on us. They were fond of children and friendly and had lots of lovely food - which we certainly did not have on our rations'. The 1944 bomb on the studios: 'I was playing tennis on the Lensbury Club tennis courts just across the street - literally within spitting distance of Warner Brother studios. The warning sounded and we heard the throb

of a V1 approaching ... the engine cut out so we slung ourselves to the ground and then came the deafening explosion and the ground seemed to heave beneath us and there was a roar as flames leapt sky high'. And D-day: 'We had heard the drone of heavy aircraft very, very early before sunrise ... when we went out in the road and looked we saw what seemed to be thousands of Dakotas going across Teddington in a south-easterly direction'.

VE Day brought great relief and massive celebrations. Some went to parties in Teddington: 'Much dancing and singing, tables laid out with food and drink, decorations and flag waving, and living near Bushy Park we had some of the Americans join in the fun'. Others went to London, and Buckingham Palace in particular: 'Walking, walking all round - outside the palace cheering for Churchill etc'. London was lit up again. Piccadilly Circus, Nelson's Column and Big Ben became visible at night for the first time in five years.

BOMB DAMAGE AT THE NPL 29 NOVEMBER 1940 ZZZ05496 (NPL Archives)

THE AMERICAN CAMP IN BUSHY PARK

GENERAL EISENHOWER BRIEFING AT SHAEF, BUSHY PARK
c1942 ZZZ05523 (Courtesy of the Imperial War Museum)

SHAEF OFFICES IN BUSHY PARK 1943
ZZZ05524 (© The Royal Parks)

The USA Eighth Army HQ was set up in Bushy Park in 1942 as Camp Griffis (named after the first American pilot casualty of the war) as part of the plan to relieve Western Europe. This involved digging and cutting up the park as huts were built, most of them beside the Sandy Lane wall between Teddington and Hampton Wick, but some stretching towards Chestnut Avenue. The camp had an airstrip at the Hampton Wick end. Officers were billeted on local residents. When General Eisenhower was appointed to head the Allied Expeditionary Force he took against the initial Grosvenor Square location, and decided to set up his HQ in Bushy Park. It was here that the detailed planning for the invasion of Italy and D-Day took place. The conditions were spartan, with limited heating; SHAEF was kept that way to simulate real life in a European winter once the invasion had taken place. The camp stayed long after the war to meet the Cold War requirements of the Berlin Airlift and action in the Far East. The SHAEF Gate on Sandy Lane is named after the occupation of the park, and there are memorial stones to General Eisenhower's office and some of the huts.

CHAPTER FOUR

MODERN TIMES

BRITAIN EMERGED from the war effort in need of a substantial recovery programme - rebuilding its bombed cities, transferring from a war economy to peacetime production, and repaying debt. The electorate had also unexpectedly, but decisively, voted in a Labour government with a clear mandate to secure full employment and establish a welfare state. It took over a decade before there was stability and the paths of steady economic growth and social security were established. Although the 1959 General Election was won by Harold Macmillan on a 'you never had it so good' slogan after the average weekly wage hit £20 a week, it was not until the 1960s that people actually felt better off, with rationing well in the past, mod cons in the home, widespread car ownership, and foreign holidays. Teddington's post-war adjustment was not as difficult as elsewhere. The story of the latter part of the 20th century was one of increasing wealth, a different profile of employment, tensions as new ideas for running public services and businesses emerged, and changing lifestyles.

The major war damage was on Church Road and at the junction of Stanley Road with Hampton Road. The immediate response was the erection of temporary housing. A three-stage development plan was approved in 1956. The first stage - clearing and redeveloping the bombed area between Stanley Road, Somerset Road, and Church Road, and rebuilding the Methodist Church - had been achieved by the early 1960s. The other stages of the plan were more or less carried out subsequently, if rather later than intended. The move of

St Mary's and St Peter's School (the long-term successor of the original Teddington Public School) from the Broad Street end of Church Road to its current site half way up Church Road took place in 1979. The redevelopment of the area on the north side of Broad Street where it meets Stanley Road was begun in the 1980s, providing a new line of shops and a housing estate in the vacant space left by the war damage.

50 ELMFIELD AVENUE 2005 ZZZ05497 (Vicky Higgin)

Some reconstruction of war damage was fairly immediate (this house, demolished in 1940, was rebuilt in 1943); most was not.

The major housing developments were of a different nature. As the London and local middle classes grew, with an increasing desire for owner occupation and the money and job security to finance it, Teddington became an attractive location. The large Harrowdene Gardens estate was built between the railway line and Sandy Lane; other substantial modern estates appeared along Cromwell Road after Bridgeman School was demolished, at various points off Broom Road, and along Twickenham Road. There were smaller developments as large old houses and bungalows were replaced by modern houses and apartment blocks. With renting diminishing there was some gentrification in the older streets, but not on the scale of that occurring in Inner London suburbs. Because much of Teddington had been built before the motor car era, the streets often have two lines of parked cars; a lot of the controversy over new housing centred on car access and traffic.

The younger and newer residents of Teddington had different lifestyles from their pre-war and immediately post-war predecessors. There were more women in the workforce, and they often continued to work or resumed work within a few years after having children (the days when women had to relinquish their jobs in the Civil Service upon marriage were very distant). There were freezers as well as fridges in the home, and a new set of electric goods to acquire. Shopping for food and other basic provisions became more of a once-a-week rather than daily effort, and often done using the car. This trend, together with the emergence of off-the-peg chain stores for men's suits, spelt the inevitable decline of the individual food stores, tailors, and drapers that had made up much of the basis of Broad Street and the High Street.

On Broad Street, supermarket shopping arrived with the opening of a large Tesco in 1971 - later it expanded its car parking

THE LAST MAJOR LONDON FOG

London fogs were renowned. For two centuries they had occurred almost every autumn and winter, and they featured in Dickens's books and other Victorian novels. Teddington, being on the river, was literally in the thick of them. The over-sixties will remember the dense grey air, buses suddenly looming out of nowhere, the yellow sulphurous wisps of smoke, and schools closing early (hooray!). The 1952 London fog was estimated to have killed over 4,000 people; it prompted the Clean Air Acts that ended commercial emission and domestic open fires. The last major fog occurred in December 1962. Teddington commuters had the odd experience of entering the transport system in dense fog and emerging into clearer air in Central London, where the changes following the Acts had already been fully implemented.

facilities. Many smaller shops were able to survive this, and may even have benefited from the attraction of Tesco. When Sainsbury's opened its store at St Clares, Hampton two miles away, with a very large car park and opening hours stretching into the evening and Sundays, the competition proved too strong and one by one the small independent food shops disappeared. In their place emerged enterprises that covered new markets - freezer food, TV rentals, cafes and takeaways, a modern sportswear shop, electronics, cameras, and more recently charity shops. Not all of these have survived, but many had or have had 20-year lives. Building societies also set up branches, and the first one (Alliance and Leicester) was graced with a mayorial opening. In the 1980s the architecture of the north side of Broad Street was altered. Towards the railway bridge end, St Peter's and St Paul's Church was demolished; it was replaced in 1980 by flats with large shops at street level (currently occupied by Boots, a video rental and furniture stores). On the opposite side of Church Road the new St Peter's and St Paul's Church and some modern flats were constructed. At the Hampton Road end of Broad Street, the advertising boards masking the open spaces to the north of Broad Street were taken down at last when the new shops and housing estate appeared.

The changes on the High Street were of a different nature. While it was normal to walk across the railway bridge or take the car to shop at Tesco, there was far less reason to do so in the reverse direction. The High Street

THE OLD ST PETER'S AND ST PAUL'S CHURCH c1865
ZZZ05498 (Richmond upon Thames Local Studies Collection)

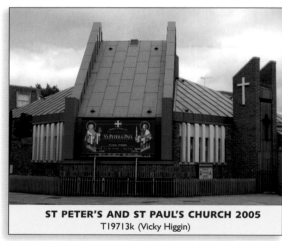

ST PETER'S AND ST PAUL'S CHURCH 2005
T19713k (Vicky Higgin)

experienced a period of decline in the 1970s. The resolution was unexpected. Antique and art shops replaced the old shops, and there was an increase in the number of estate agents. The really major change started in 1974 when Spaghetti Junction, a pizza parlour, opened opposite Lloyds Bank and quickly established a market. This led over the next two decades to restaurants and cafes opening up all along the High Street to meet a new demand for eating out, and for the different types of food that had become popular thanks to foreign holidays and the growth in ethnic communities. The pubs had to respond. The traditional ones declined, and others began to raise the standard of their food and host foreign restaurants. This was not specifically planned (at one time a councillor objected to yet another catering establishment - he was concerned that the Via Veneto was coming to the High Street), but Teddington may have been the better for it. The High Street became a livelier place in the evenings, and al fresco eating on the street or along opened frontages became possible in the summer months.

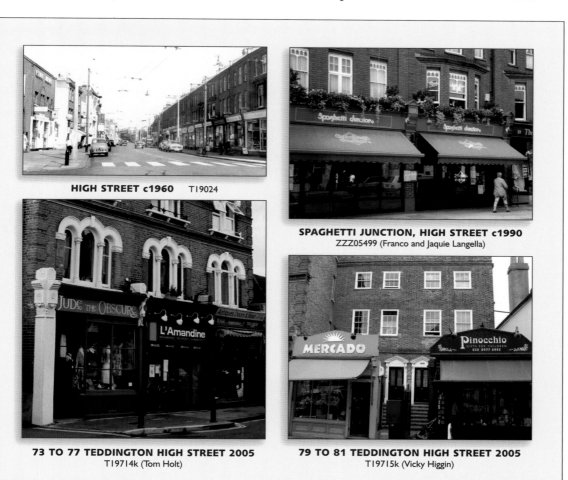

HIGH STREET c1960 T19024

SPAGHETTI JUNCTION, HIGH STREET c1990
ZZZ05499 (Franco and Jaquie Langella)

73 TO 77 TEDDINGTON HIGH STREET 2005
T19714k (Tom Holt)

79 TO 81 TEDDINGTON HIGH STREET 2005
T19715k (Vicky Higgin)

These four pictures of the High Street show how it changed. In 1960 the trolley bus wires were still there, but the architecture of this end of the High Street is unchanged. Spaghetti Junction grew in the 1980s to a large establishment. At the same time, the shops further down changed to antique shops, art shops and cafes, and some of them are still sited in what were the front gardens of Georgian or Victorian houses.

Fact File

MILLERS THE BUTCHERS, WALDEGRAVE ROAD 2005 T19716k (Vicky Higgin)

There has been a butcher's shop at 152 Waldegrave Road since it was built in the first decade of the 20th century. The current proprieter, Andy Miller, has bucked the closure trend elsewhere by specialising in meat from free-range farms and without preservatives, and is Teddington's last remaining independent butcher. His custom is from an area wider than Teddington. The queues for turkeys, geese, hams and other seasonal meat (with mince pies, coffee and spiced tea on offer while you wait) are part of his customers' Christmas tradition.

The three local employers that had featured in the wartime effort were able to modify their operations after the war, but each faced major challenges in the final 20 years of the century. For the NPL, now employing over 1,000 staff, the end of the war work meant that their programmes and effort could be diverted to exploiting and regulating the technologies that had emerged during the war. In the years that followed, the NPL was able to notch up a significant number of firsts. Alan Turing, regarded by many as the father of modern computing, moved from his wartime work in the Bletchley code-breaking operation to pioneer a fast UK computer; although overtaken by American work in the commercial field, the NPL subsequently retained a leading role in scientific and mathematical computing. The 'packet switching' telecommunications technology that underpins computer networks and the Internet was first developed by an NPL team. The use of the atomic clock as the basis for precise time measurement was also started at the NPL. Amongst the NPL's other programmes, there was support for the new hovercraft, advice on structures where wind resistance is a key factor (such as the Post Office Tower), the shape of wings for military and commercial aircraft, and support to healthcare in the use of X-ray

and ultra-violet light technology; also, with the recent concerns over climate change, the development of measures and standards for air pollution.

In wartime there had been a natural focus and unity about the work of the NPL. In peacetime, getting the scale right and balancing the priority between routine calibration and standards, specific projects for industry or the military, and guided innovative research, has always been less easy; this has preoccupied directors of the NPL and those responsible for its governance. This has led to changes in its institutional structure. In 1965, British Calibration Services was founded so that instead of NPL doing the testing, industry did it on an accredited basis.

THE PILOT ACE COMPUTER BEFORE COMPLETION 1950 ZZZ05500 (NPL Archives)

More fundamental reform came with the new approaches for managing the public sector that emerged in the 1980s. The shipping side was hived off and privatised as the National Maritime Institute in 1982, and the Computer Aided Design Centre was also privatised. The core NPL became an 'arms-length' Executive Agency in 1991, and moved to its current 'Government owned, commercially operated' structure in 1995. The DTI hold the land and the physical infrastructure, and are responsible for the investment programmes for them. The operations are run by NPL Management as part of Serco Ltd. As a result of these steps, the number of staff directly employed by NPL Management was reduced to around 600. However, from Teddington's employment viewpoint the overall numbers on the sites are still above 1,000. The privatised National Maritime Institute still operates from here, and NPL Management's various subcontractors mainly work on site. In 1988 the Laboratory of the Government Chemist moved alongside,

relocating from cramped and expensive premises in Central London. The choice of Teddington was influenced by the links to NPL work. Their main programmes include work on alcohol and tobacco in connection with health issues and excise duties, analysis for forensic work including control of drugs, and an increasing portfolio on public health support and pollution advice.

Tough's boatyard reverted to peacetime production with a reduced labour force. As well as more routine production of small craft, a number of prestigious assignments came their way, including craft for the films 'Moby Dick', 'A Man for All Seasons', 'Dr Zhivago', and 'Anthony and Cleopatra'; the 'Havengore' barge used for Sir Winston Churchill's funeral; and craft for the Queen's 1977 Silver Jubilee celebrations. Douglas Tough was elected President of the Ship and Boat Builders Federation in 1951. Business dropped after 1970, and the boatyard closed in the late 1980s.

Fact File

An unusual occurance at Teddington lock (I)

The foundation stone of 1857 had been submerged, and it disappeared. It was found again during refurbishment of the lock in 1952, and restored as a memorial on the walls of the lock house.

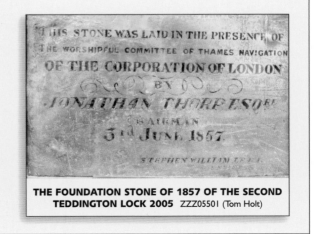

THE FOUNDATION STONE OF 1857 OF THE SECOND TEDDINGTON LOCK 2005 ZZZ05501 (Tom Holt)

Teddington Studios was reopened by Danny Kaye in 1948 after reconstruction of the site. However, from 1951 British film production went into sharp decline for a variety of commercial and political reasons. Recovery came from a different source. With the advent of ITV in 1955 to challenge BBC's initial TV monopoly position, a need arose for TV production sites, and in 1958 ABC decided on Teddington Studios for theirs (which transferred to Thames TV from 1968). Over 30 years some of the most successful series were produced here, including 'The Avengers', 'The World at War', 'The Sweeney', 'Minder', and 'Rumpole'. There were also situation comedy series filmed here, such as 'For the Love of Ada', 'Bless this House', and 'George and Mildred'; the detective series 'Callan' and 'Van der Valk'; and general light entertainment programmes such as 'Opportunity Knocks' and 'The Eammon Andrews Show'. New rules came in for the allocation of franchises for ITV, and

Fact File

A major threat to Teddington suspension bridge occurred in 1964. From early in the morning of Sunday 23 February, teenage girls flocked to the bridge; word had got out that the Beatles would be coming to Teddington Studios. The Beatles arrived on a police launch. As they embarked into a decorated car for the short distance from the lock to the studios, one girl managed to break the barrier. She sat on one of the Beatles' lap before landing in the less welcome arms of the police, as the Beatles obtained sanctuary in the foyer.

THE BEATLES AT TEDDINGTON STUDIOS 1964 ZZZ05506
(Courtesy of the Editor, Richmond and Twickenham Times)

PLAQUES ON THE WALL OF TEDDINGTON STUDIOS 2005 ZZZ05503, ZZZ05504, ZZZ05505 (Tom Holt)

These are three of eleven plaques commemorating stars of TV comedy series made at Teddington Studios. Benny Hill lived in Teddington.

Fact File

An unusual occurance at Teddington lock (II)

The fish-slapping dance involving John Cleese and Michael Palin in 'Monty Python's Flying Circus' occurred on Teddington Lock. This historic confrontation has its own blue memorial plaque in the window of the measuring tower and a signed memento in the lock house. As a result there is considerable USA and Japanese interest in Teddington Lock.

A MEMENTO OF THE FISH SLAPPING DANCE
ZZZ05502 (Teddington Lock Keepers)

in 1992 Thames lost the London franchise to Carlton. This was a sharp blow to immediate local employment, as the permanent production staff were drastically reduced. There was still production activity on a contracted basis, and the studios were the setting for some major TV series including 'Birds of a Feather', 'Goodnight Sweetheart', and 'Men Behaving Badly', as well as for the continuation of 'Minder' and 'The Bill'. Recently Teddington Studios was absorbed into Pinewood Studios.

As well as the changes for these employers, Teddington experienced the general trend away from manufacturing industry. The coal yard by the station was closed down and replaced by Teddington Business Park for small enterprises. When the Savoy Cinema closed, it was replaced by an office block, Harlequin House, initially taken by the AA and now by a number of smaller businesses. Haymarket Publishing took over premises on Hampton Road.

Following a period of stability after the post-war changes had settled down, both the education and health care services became subject of political battle.

The Education Act of 1902 had brought Teddington within Middlesex County Council. The history of education in Teddington to 1944 was one of gradually expanding capacity to reflect the increasing population and the general extension of the age at which pupils left school. Stanley Road School appeared in 1907, St Mark's School in 1927 (on the site now occupied by Sacred Heart School), and steadily the senior pupils were located in Stanley Road for boys and Victoria Church of England School (on Princes Road but closed in 1960) for girls as well as at St Mark's School. The curriculum was an extension of elementary schoolwork, not secondary education as we now know it.

The 1944 Butler Education Acts which were to be implemented by the incoming 1945 Labour Government required the provision of full secondary education for all to age 15 (raised to 16 in 1965). The implementation followed the pattern elsewhere, with the 11-plus separation of pupils between grammar, technical and secondary modern schools. By 1964 the state sector for Teddington was offering three local secondary moderns, with grammar school opportunities at Hampton Grammar for boys and Twickenham County for girls. The 1960s Labour governments wanted an end to selection at the age of 11 and sought local plans for implementing their policy. After the reorganisation of local government, the task of responding fell to the new London Borough of Richmond. This was bound to divide the community, as there were strongly felt arguments on both sides of the debate on the end of grammar schools. The first proposals were politically controversial. The scheme put forward by the Conservative-controlled council was for the retention of the borough's grammar schools and the upgrading of the secondary moderns to 'bilateral schools' with stronger academic streams and viable sixth forms; selection at 11 would be based on 'guided parental' views and a recommendation from primary school rather than a one-day exam. It was no surprise when the Secretary of State, Anthony Crosland, rejected the proposals.

The ground was conceded over the next few years against the political reality of central government policy and strong and well articulated pressure from some parents, who did not want their children to be in the 'disadvantaged' 65% who did not get into grammar school by whatever means 11-plus selection was governed. The 1971 proposals were radical, and were set out on the basis of three tiers - locally based primary schools, local comprehensives for ages 11-16, and two sixth form colleges for 16- to 18-year-olds. The proposals were accepted by the Secretary of State for the new government, Margaret Thatcher, and were implemented with full commitment from 1973. In the subsequent decade the two sixth form colleges and Twickenham College of Technology were merged to form Richmond upon Thames College, London's first tertiary college, which provided a curriculum that ran across the full range of academic and vocational 16-18 education.

For Teddington there was a final piece of the jigsaw to complete. While 'girls only' schools remained popular, 'boys only' schools were not, and particularly so for one situated geographically on the edge of the borough. The prospect of declining numbers, forcing more boys to go to the single-sex Teddington School, and girls having to cross the river to Grey Court to get to a mixed school, led to the decision to make Teddington School a mixed school from 1984.

TEDDINGTON SCHOOL, BROOM ROAD 2005 T19717k (Tom Holt)

While the political focus was on the secondary front, the primary schools were steadily acquiring more modern premises. Collis School moved to Fairfax Road with extensive grounds in 1972, and St Mary's and St Peters moved to their new site further up Church Road in 1979.

There had always been an active private education sector in Teddington, with several schools in existence in Victorian times. Between the wars, Summerleigh, a boarding school for girls on Hampton Road run by a Swiss-born principal, and Twickenham Grammar on Waldegrave Park (where Newlands House is now), were significant institutions. Lady Eleanor Holles School opened in nearby Hampton in 1937 after a temporary stay in the old Summerleigh premises. This substantially expanded the private sector. The ending of council responsibility for maintenance of Hampton Grammar after the comprehensive system had been put in place and subsequent ending of direct grant funding of places made the school entirely private. Whether this was the intention or not, the private sector became stronger and more focused, with the local preparatory level schools feeding into the academically successful schools in Hampton or further afield into the Latymer and St Paul's schools in Hammersmith and Barnes.

Following the end of the war in Vietnam, some of the Vietnamese unaccompanied refugee children (often referred to as boat children) came to live in Teddington under the auspices of Save the Children. At first, from 1982, they lived in Hampton Court House. They were later dispersed to smaller houses. The Teddington-based houses were in Queens Road and Waldegrave Park. They were educated in local schools, and most went on to Richmond upon Thames College. 20 went on to university education and later settled into IT, scientific and NHS professions. The Vietnamese New Year celebrations are a highlight of the calendar, with staged events and festival food. An office of the South West London Vietnamese Association is in Church Road, and acts as a community centre for the children and some of the parents who later joined them.

CHILDREN READY FOR THE VIETNAMESE NEW YEAR CELEBRATION 2003 ZZZ05507
(SW London Vietnamese Association)

The creation of the NHS was one of the most far-reaching, radical and enduring measures taken by the 1945-51 Labour governments. The three years of transition from 1945 to 1948 were difficult for Teddington's hospital with the ending of war time subsidies, the need to consult on many matters, and handling the transition to being part of a national physiotherapy department, an up-to-date patient records office, a consultant's suite and modern wards. A League of Friends had been set up in 1954, and through their efforts and the generous donations of individuals and local organizations there were funds for investment to supplement those provided by the state.

TEDDINGTON MEMORIAL HOSPITAL 1988 ZZZ05508 (Gwendoline Smith, League of Friends of Teddington Hospital)

institution. Those responsible for the hospital were proud of the fact that in the end they had balanced the books and were transferring the hospital in 'a first class condition'. The hospital did not do particularly well in terms of NHS investment allocations, and it took until 1976 before the hospital had acquired ward day rooms, a complete purpose-built

Small hospitals such as Teddington's did not fit easily into the NHS pattern emerging in the 1960s and 1970s of GPs covering primary care and large District General Hospitals and University Teaching Hospitals handling secondary care and Accident and Emergency. However, the proposal to close the hospital did not stem from a careful analysis of the options for balancing care facilities; rather, it arose as reaction to a financial crisis and muddled administrational arrangements that could not cope. The decision to align Local Authority and Health Authority boundaries had led to an anomaly whereby there was no major hospital in the borough of Richmond other than at Roehampton on its eastern edge. As a compromise solution, Twickenham and Teddington Hospitals were administered from outside the borough by Hounslow and Spelthorne District Health Authority. When West Middlesex Hospital made heavy financial overruns, and simultaneously 'efficiency savings' were called for by central government in the early 1980s, the District Health Authority decided to resolve the crisis by closing the Twickenham and Teddington hospitals.

It did not prove to be as easy as that. The local communities protested, and the 54,000 signatures between them made an impressive impact. The local MP, Toby Jessel, was fully supportive of the campaign against closure, and took every opportunity to raise the issue in the House of Commons. When the District and Regional Health Authorities confirmed their intention to close the hospitals, the issue was raised all the way to the Minister for Health. A 24-hour candle-lit vigil at the hospital led by Pam Bryant of the League of Friends, a resolute constituency MP, further mounds of protest signatures, the clear support of the local press, and a defeat linked to the protest in two local by-elections (which led to the first ever change in power at the council) were substantial

pressures. Nevertheless, the outcome was in doubt to the very end. In December 1983 the Minister for Health, Kenneth Clark, decided to retain Teddington's hospital (but not its operating theatre) and to close Twickenham's hospital. With the hospital's future assured, it was possible to invest again. Wards were modernised and a new one built; a new X-ray department with equipment was established; and there were new facilities for patients and staff. Once again a very substantial proportion of the money came thanks to the Teddington public raising money, as in the 1920s, for many of the improvements. With national policy moving from centralised planning to local responsiveness, Teddington Hospital was successful in its application to become a Trust under the early 1990s reforms of the NHS; it became the smallest NHS Trust in England.

PAM BRYANT STARTS THE VIGIL AT TEDDINGTON HOSPITAL 1983 ZZZ05509
(League of Friends of Teddington Hospital)

NORMANSFIELD HOSPITAL c1990 ZZZ05476 (Miriam Bruinsma Internet Gallery)

Another Teddington hospital came to national attention in the latter part of the century and hit the headlines for all the wrong reasons. The Langdon-Down family had run Normansfield Hospital until 1951, when rising costs made it no longer possible to continue to do so as a private home. It was transferred relatively smoothly to the NHS. There was subsequent investment, aided by a League of Friends, with new day rooms, improved lighting and heating and better staff accommodation. The centenary celebrations in 1968 brought welcome publicity, and there appeared to be nothing untoward when the final Langdon-Down member of staff retired in 1971.

In 1976 Normansfield staff went on strike in protest at the regime run by the then consultant psychologist, Dr Lawlor. In terms of immediate impact it was successful - Dr Lawlor was suspended and an independent inquiry was launched. When the inquiry reported eighteen months later, the national headlines were devastating: 'Doctor's Hell Hospital' was just one example. There was no doubt in the inquiry's report where most of the blame lay; the conclusion was that Dr Lawlor had run an intolerant, abusive and tyrannical regime. There was also criticism of the hospital and area administrators, the low standards of nursing care and training (but there was no evidence of cruelty), the filthy state of parts of the hospital, including the catering areas, and the bare and depressing wards.

At a national level, the Normansfield Inquiry led to changes in policy development for the mentally handicapped and the strengthening of inspection regimes, and raised difficult issues over the right to strike in the NHS where patient care could be affected.

Locally, the management and staff had to pick up the pieces. There was significant investment from the NHS and the League of Friends, who provided a new day centre, a recreation club and a hydrotherapy pool. In 1981, when the new £1.3m complex was officially opened by Sir George Young, a Health Minister, there had been sufficient recovery and investment to allow him to claim that Normansfield was again leading the way. During a subsequent period of financial savings in the NHS in the 1980s, the Friends (led by the actor Brian Rix) paid for extra staff to ensure satisfactory care. The patients had more fulfilling opportunities on site (and off site for the more advanced), and there were fun days and seaside holidays. Nevertheless, this was still care in an institutional setting, and not all the dormitories or facilities had been upgraded.

Care in the Community became national policy for the mentally handicapped in the late 1980s. In some respects, this was a confirmation and extension of the Langdon-Down philosophy that they had the potential to lead rewarding lives (albeit with different opportunities and challenges) if appropriately supported. This was enacted in the subsequent decade, with Normansfield closing in 1996. After much debate, most of the grounds went to residential housing. The main building remains. Part of it houses the Langdon-Down Centre Trust, who let two of the floors to the Down's Syndrome Association. The theatre is preserved with its stock of scenery, and is used for conferences, meetings, and occasional fund-raising performances. There are plans for a permanent exhibition of Dr Langdon-Down's life and work and Normansfield history.

THE NEW RESIDENTS' CLUB AT NORMANSFIELD
c1990 ZZZ05479 (Miriam Bruinsma Internet Gallery)

Alongside these serious education and health care events, there was less controversy and much progress in Teddington's sports and the enhancement of its leisure facilities.

The war had interrupted sporting life. Not only were the participants dispersed in the armed forces, but the grounds themselves were affected. The playing fields at Lensbury were not the only victims. In Bushy Park the hockey and cricket pitch had been used for allotments, and there were paths across the reserve pitches. The pavilion had also burnt down after a fire on VJ Day. Teams were forced to play away, and it was two or three years before sporting life returned to normal.

Teddington Hockey Club was able to celebrate its centenary still in the top flight of a sport that had remained avowedly amateur. It enjoyed a period of great success in the 1990s, winning the National Hockey League in 1994-95 and the Cup in 1993-94 and 1996-97, and went on to represent England in Europe. Teddington players were members of all the Great Britain teams from

Fact File

It was usual until the 1960s for offices to work on Saturday morning. Teddington Hockey Club players used to go to Victoria Station to find out which team they were playing for and where to go. Teddington Town Cricket Club, which had been formed from St Peter's and St Paul's Church members, had many traders in its ranks and ran a Wednesday XI which at its peak was stronger than the weekend teams.

THE CENTENARY PHOTO OF TEDDINGTON HOCKEY CLUB 1971 ZZZ05517 (Teddington Hockey Club

the 1992 Barcelona Olympics to the 2004 Athens Olympics. Rather belatedly, in 1990 a women's section was formed, which has grown and now reached the South League.

Teddington Cricket Club also saw success in this period. In the 1980s and 1990s it won the Middlesex County Cricket League and the Middlesex Cup on several occasions, and the National Club Championship in 1987, 1989 and 1991. The separate Teddington Town Cricket Club faced difficulty when its pavilion burnt down in 1970. It merged with its winter tenants, the Antlers Rugby Club, to form Teddington Town Sports Club with a new pavilion.

converted to all-year sports surfaces, and Teddington Sports Club opened. Teddington Hockey Club use the pitches, as the sport has moved to using synthetic surfaces, and a club house is in prospect. As the corporate climate changed to a less paternalistic one, the status of the Lensbury Club was altered, first by separating out the BP connection, and then by an 'arms-length' relationship with Shell. The company eventually sold the sports grounds, but retained the main building as a hotel and conference centre. It opened up membership of the Lensbury Club and hire of the facilities to the general public in 1999.

SAILING AT TAMESIS CLUB 2005 T19720k (Tom Holt)

A couple of juniors sailing on a quiet Sunday at Tamesis.

The sporting facilities open to the public were enhanced. Teddington Swimming Baths were rebuilt in 1977 to become enclosed with modern changing facilities. Later a gym was added. The land at the back of Teddington School and part of its playground was

On the river, the Royal Canoe Club took the opportunity of acquiring the premises on the adjacent mainland from BP, and the Walbrook Rowing Club, previously part of BP, also came into it. The skiff club also came across from Kingston.

TROWLOCK ISLAND 2005 T19718k (Tom Holt)

Access to Trowlock Island is by barge, not always convenient for the members of the Canoe Club.

The facilities expanded to cover a full range, with sections for canoes, kayaks, rowing, skiffs, and outriggers. Tamesis has also widened its activities as new types of sailing vessels have appeared. Some members have become prominent in national and international yachting bodies, and have represented Great Britain in the Olympic Games.

Teddington had taken steps to preserve its architecture with a limit on developments on the High Street and Broad Street. The threat to it came from a different direction. The crowds of worshippers at St Alban's in the Edwardian period had masked an underlying trend. A church attendance census in 1902 indicated that while Teddington's population had grown tenfold in the previous 50 years, church attendance had grown at just half that rate. In the inter-war years there was still a congregation to match the scale of the building, and in 1936 St Mary's reopened as a chapel of ease to St Alban's. Attendance declined in the post-war years, and by the 1960s the cost of maintaining two churches so close to each other had become a burden for the Diocese.

In November 1972 Jean Brown, then a councillor, spotted a small item on the planning committee agenda proposing to close St Alban's Church. 'This was the first

time I had heard such a thing. I worshipped there and, to my knowledge, no-one in the congregation had any idea that the building would be closed.' She began the campaign to prevent this happening, and the likely consequence of the demolition of the building.

The first effort ended in failure. When the Church Commissioners announced their intention to make St Alban's redundant, Jean appealed to the Judicial Committee of the Privy Council and took the battle all the way to Downing Street, where her appeal was rejected in 1976. The church was closed in

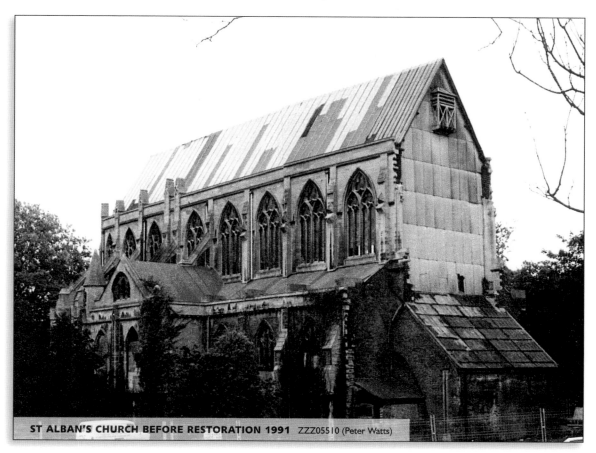

ST ALBAN'S CHURCH BEFORE RESTORATION 1991 ZZZ05510 (Peter Watts)

ST ALBAN'S CHURCH AFTER RESTORATION 2005 ZZZ05511 (Graham Watson)

1977, and St Mary's (renamed the Church of St Mary with St Alban) became the parish church again. Nevertheless, the exercise had been helpful in preventing any swift premature action.

The abandoned church became a target for vandalism and occasional squatters, and its fabric began to suffer. The floors were torn up, some of the windows were shattered, and fittings were removed or defaced. It was regarded by the Diocese as its worst redundant church. In 1981 plans to convert the building to squash courts, a shop, a sauna and an office block were put forward and

were rejected by the council. In the next year a man called Colin Waters (who claimed that he was asked to do it) was caught stripping copper from the roof and jailed. These events re-ignited the campaign to save St Alban's. It began again at the church on a freezing November day in 1985 amid the debris, damaged fittings and dead pigeons. The campaign had the backing of the council, the local newspapers, and crucially many of the people of Teddington, who signed up in their hundreds. In 1986 a public enquiry began considering the two alternatives put to it: either to completely demolish the church, or to retain it, converting it to flats with others surrounding it. The campaign was successful. The church was saved, and the Secretary of State's concluded that 'St Alban's well deserves its II* grading by virtue of its architectural interest and its importance as a prominent feature of the Teddington area.' This reflected what Teddington residents, religious or otherwise, had felt, and the unexpected discovery of the upgrading was welcome, as it meant that the church would stay intact with no major internal alteration.

The next few years were rewarding ones.

English Heritage and the Diocese provided funds to restore the church, with a new roof, proper bricking at the west end, and three new stained glass windows. The architecture of the new Cloister Close flats that emerged nearby blended well with the church, and the High Street and the church hall were refurbished. There was much to celebrate in 1989 on the centenary of the opening of St Alban's. In 1995 a new era started for the building as the home of the Landmark Arts Centre, of which Jean Brown is the Honorary President.

JEAN BROWN UNVEILS THE PLAQUE TO HERSELF AT THE LANDMARK ARTS CENTRE 2002
ZZZ05512 (Courtesy of Jean Brown)

TEDDINGTON at the start of the 21st century is not expected to change greatly. Nor does anybody particularly want it to. With the riverfront, the parks, the character of the High Street, and generally two- or three-storey housing, this is an environment to be preserved for those who live and work in Teddington. That does not mean that nothing changes, or that parts of Teddington are museum pieces and are to be treated as such. In its most historic area by the river and the two church buildings there is real activity.

St Mary's Church (now called St Mary with St Alban) is once again the active parish church. It has a congregation of around 350, of which half are regular and active members. The church retains its history with the memorial stones to Stephen Hales and other historic Teddington residents; it is of interest to tourists, particularly from the USA, owing to Stephen Hales's reputation there. It has also taken in the surviving religious artefacts from St Alban's. But it is first and foremost a live church, furnished and laid out for active Christian worship by the local community with attention to children and younger members. There is a choir, a Sunday school, and full use of the church hall over the road. The graveyard has an open aspect, and the new Cloister Close flats provide an appropriate backcloth; it is kept tidy, and is properly cared for as part of the community's environment.

ST MARY'S CHURCH AND GRAVEYARD 2005 T19719k (Tom Holt)

A CONCERT AT THE LANDMARK ARTS CENTRE 2005 ZZZ05513 (John Ovett)

The decision to use the large St Alban's Church for an arts centre has been vindicated. At its tenth anniversary, the Landmark Arts Centre has seen success. Its Art Fairs have gained a reputation across the south of England; there are interesting concerts, and the venue has been used by many local choirs; and there is a flourishing education and children's programme. There have also been a couple of major occasions. 'Elizabeth' was filmed here, and the borough chose the Landmark for its cross-borough performances of the Verdi Requiem in 2000 to celebrate the new millennium and commemorate the centenary of the composer's death.

Teddington Lock now sees very little commercial river traffic. Its leisure users cover the full range - from tourist cruises between Richmond and Hampton Court to yachts and small craft of all descriptions. On any weekend there are walkers, runners, and cyclists passing through, or coming and going over the suspension bridge, and in summer the site is busy with people eating outside in the café on the Ham side and at the Anglers on the Teddington side. Upstream there is angling, and the Royal Canoe Club have one of the most attractive stretches of the river as their course, running from Teddington to Hampton Court.

THE WOODLAND GARDENS 2005 T19721k (Tom Holt)

Bushy Park received money from the Heritage Lottery Fund to plan a major restoration. At the time of writing the Diana (or Arethusa) Fountain is having its stonework repaired and its bronze restored. There are projects in train to enhance the Woodland Gardens with particular features such as a Japanese-style amphitheatre, as well as improved paths and watercourses. From a historic viewpoint, the proposal to restore the gardens at Upper Lodge to public use and recover the ponds and the 18th-century cascade between them is of particular interest.

The attractiveness of Teddington's environment is probably the primary threat to it. There is little room for major housing development in a part of London that is expected to grow over the next two decades. It is not surprising, then, that by that most

THE WOODLAND GARDENS 2005 T19722k (Tom Holt)

THE DIANA FOUNTAIN, BUSHY PARK c2000
ZZZ05467 (Courtesy of the Royal Parks)

discussed metric - house prices - Teddington remains a highly valued residential location (in one survey it was reckoned to have had the highest price rise in London over the fifteen years from 1990). The pressure to build upwards or more densely is carefully controlled. Under the Civil Amenities Act and subsequent legislation, there are six conservation areas: the Lock, the High Street, the Grove, part of Broom Water, the area between Park Road and the railway line north of Clarence Road, and Blackmores Grove. There are proposals to extend some of these and to preserve particular houses within them. The major housing developments occur when a large local institution or enterprise closes.

THE VIEW FROM TEDDINGTON SUSPENSION FOOTBRIDGE 2005 T19723k (Tom Holt)

The two most recent have been on what was the site of Tough's boatyard and Normansfield Hospital. The first has seen some smart modern apartment blocks on the riverside (following a scare that a supermarket plus car park might be placed on the river front). The second has been the site of a new housing estate of luxury two- or three-storey homes. Elsewhere, developments have been on a smaller scale, with large old houses and gardens being replaced by more densely packed houses or in some cases by crescents.

There is no need for estate agent hype in selling Teddington to families. The evidence is there, with the primary schools heavily oversubscribed at the time of writing. Collis School will be substantially expanded to cope with three-class entry, which is double the intake of just fifteen years ago. The comprehensive system for the state schools has been stable since its introduction, and the choice at state secondary level is one that parents in other parts of London would be delighted with. At the age of sixteen pupils have the choice of Richmond upon Thames College with its unrivalled width of curriculum and good academic results, or crossing the river to Esher or Kingston Colleges. Some celebrities have passed through the local system: Andrew Gilligan, the journalist at the heart of the Iraq weapons of mass destruction episode, and Keira Knightley, the actress, are among them.

Fact File

CRAIG HALL 2005 T19724k (Tom Holt)

23 and 23A Clarence Road are a recent conversion of Craig Hall. Originating in 1859 as the meeting place for Methodists, it later became the meeting place for Baptists until they moved to Church Road. In the 20th century it had a variety of uses - as a court house, a playgroup centre, and a Teddington Theatre Club location. The conversion preserved the frontage.

Teddington Memorial Hospital now fits with the grain of current national policies of local responsiveness in health care services. Since the millennium there has been a transformation. A major £1million investment funded by the League of Friends has bought a modern X-ray department equipped with a high technology PACS (Picture Archiving and Communication System) only available elsewhere in much larger hospitals, together with a purpose-built and equipped rehabilitation unit. This became the basis for the hospital to contain an NHS Walk-In Centre and pharmacy, which was government-funded. The hospital has also benefited from government funding with new inpatient wards as part of the initiative to end 'Nightingale Wards' in hospitals. The hospital is equipped to serve the community for its non-acute health care, and is well placed for any new role that emerges as health care commissioning becomes more local. Much of this would not have occurred without the support of the community of Teddington and surrounding areas, expressed through the funding that the League of Friends have been able to put towards its achievement.

In 1973 the Teddington Society was formed with the objectives of protecting the history and character of the town, ensuring that the people of Teddington have a say in local developments, and creating a real community spirit in Teddington. It functions through working groups covering planning, roads and transport, riverside and open spaces, trees and gardens, and historical research. Some of these tasks are far from straightforward.

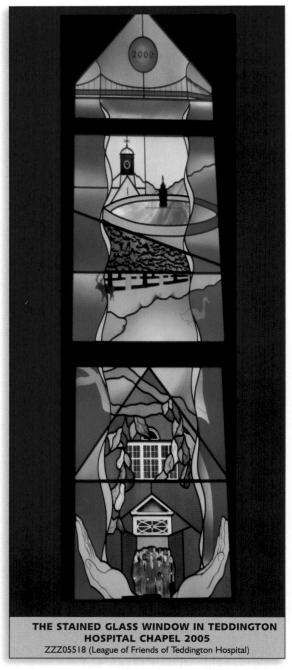

THE STAINED GLASS WINDOW IN TEDDINGTON HOSPITAL CHAPEL 2005
ZZZ05518 (League of Friends of Teddington Hospital)

At the bottom are arms which embrace the images of Teddington locations above; readers may wish to identify these.

Getting the balance right between preventing insensitive development but avoiding an attitude of freezing to the current position is never easy. Likewise, keeping Teddington tidy in a world of litter and graffiti is an uphill battle. At its Jubilee in 1998 the Teddington Society could look back with some satisfaction at its achievements. The gardens in front of Elmfield House, together with the trees and greenery on the other side of the road, have made the centre of Teddington a far pleasanter place than the previous rather bare scene by the railway bridge. The millennium book on houses in Teddington since 1800 has provided a readable and informed account. Chestnut Sunday has been revived. In 2004 John Jantzen was awarded an MBE for his unstinting work in removing graffiti and preserving the environment.

Teddington cannot be a community in the sense of a small village. Its social life expresses itself as a number of networks developed through shared experience as parents, being at school together, at sports clubs, and in religious and cultural activity. The restaurants and pubs on the High Street, and increasingly on Broad Street, are one focus for getting together. So are the events organized by the Teddington Society such as the annual Teddington in Flower, when a dozen gardens are opened to public view with the hosts varying from year to year.

THE CENTENARY OF THE MODERN TEDDINGTON LOCK 2004
ZZZ05514 (Ken Mackenzie/London's Arcadia, The Thames Landscape Strategy in Action)

The Teddington Society were not alone in having cause to celebrate in the years surrounding the millennium date. While the millennium itself did not have a specific Teddington function, with many going to Central London on packed trains to see the fireworks along the river (or for some unfortunates to sweat it out worrying whether their IT work had managed to avoid the threatened 'millennium bug' disaster), there were two major anniversaries close to it. In 2002 the NPL reached its centenary, and opened a new modern set of laboratories funded by the DTI as an expression of confidence in its future. In 2004 the centenary of the modern Teddington Lock took place. As well as the celebrations, there were practical enhancements. A start was made on repainting the suspension bridge, new moorings were created on the towpath on the Ham side, and some repairs were made to the lock.

It was the arrival of the railway that changed Teddington. It probably still is the most shared experience of those who live and work in Teddington. Like the British weather, it is always the butt of a good grumble and moan (sometimes the railway's excuses are somewhat bizarre, with delays attributed to the 'wrong sort of snow', 'leaves on the line', or on one occasion 'escaped prisoners from Wandsworth'). In recent years the reality has been one of improved service, if not speed. The old 'slam door' trains are no longer used, there is an increased provision in the morning rush hour, a new timetable has restored the fifteen-minute service from London well into the evening, and the electronic information signs actually work (most of the time). And Teddington travellers have been well served by Alan Hopgood at the ticket office, who could probably tell them the quickest and cheapest route from Teddington to Timbuctoo; he has won a Customer Service Certificate on the recommendation of Teddington customers. Whatever else is said about it, the rail link to London is still the key factor that enables residents to enjoy the environment and life in Teddington while at the same time being able to benefit from the employment and entertainment opportunities of one of the world's great capital cities.

He can sort out all your travel needs

By Colleen McDonnell

Alan Hopgood

Teddington station
ticket clerk

ALAN HOPGOOD AT TEDDINGTON STATION 2004 ZZZ05515 (Courtesy of The Editor, Richmond and Twickenham Times)

ACKNOWLEDGEMENTS

As author I would like to acknowledge the help and support provided by:

Jane Baxter, Luke Denison, and Nik Pollard at the Richmond upon Thames Local Studies Library

Dennis Rowlands and Jean Nichols at Bushy Park Archives

Sharon Wilson at the National Physical Laboratory Library and Archives

Sandra Maltby at the Langdon-Down Centre Trust.

I would like to acknowledge the work of the Borough of Twickenham Local History Society, and the Teddington Society; although not directly involved in the production of this book, their published work has been an essential and valued source.

I would like to thank Miriam Bruisma; Grant Alderson and Russell Benzies of Teddington Hockey Club; Jean Brown, Irene Sutton and Graham Watson of the Landmark Arts Centre; Judy White and the Broom Water Association; Graham Sims; and Pam Bryant of The League of Friends of Teddington Hospital, for providing information and material on particular aspects.

I would also wish to thank George Hunter and Ken Howe for reading and checking draft versions and Janet Holt and Jonathan Holzmann for assistance in the final production of the book.

The NPL photographs have been reproduced by permission of the Controller of HMSO and the Queen's Printer for Scotland.

BIBLIOGRAPHY

For specific topics and aspects:

'Medieval Teddington' by Mary Clark, Borough of Twickenham Local History Society Publications

'The Houses in Teddington AD 1800 to 2000' by Paddy Ching and Teddington Society History Research Group, Teddington History Publications

'Bushy Park Royals, Rangers and Rogues' by Kathy White and Peter Foster, Foundry Press

'The Thames, Hampton to Richmond Bridge, The Walker's Guide' by David McDowall

'Dr John Langdon-Down and the Normansfield Theatre' by John Earl, Borough of Twickenham Local History Society Publications

'The Story of Teddington's Hospitals' by L Arthur Wyatt, League of Friends of Teddington Hospital

'The Story of Teddington Studios' by John Tasker, Teddington Studios

For biographies:

'Science, Philanthropy and Religion: Stephen Hales' by David Allen, Borough of Twickenham Local History Society Publication

'The Life and Times of William IV' by Anne Somerset, Wiedenfeld and Nicholson

'Mrs Jordan's Profession' by Claire Tomalin, Viking

For digestible primary material:

The Swan and Stag Magazines 1924-34 that were written for the Teddington Hospital Fetes have many historical and period articles, available at the Richmond upon Thames Local Studies Library

The response to the Teddington Community Play on the Second World War and other reminiscence material is available in the Local Studies cabinet in Teddington Library

Francis Frith
Pioneer Victorian Photographer

Francis Frith, founder of the world-famous photographic archive, was a complex and multi-talented man. A devout Quaker and a highly successful Victorian businessman, he was philosophical by nature and pioneering in outlook. By 1855 he had already established a wholesale grocery business in Liverpool, and sold it for the astonishing sum of £200,000, which is the equivalent today of over £15,000,000. Now in his thirties, and captivated by the new science of photography, Frith set out on a series of pioneering journeys up the Nile and to the Near East.

He was the first photographer to venture beyond the sixth cataract of the Nile. Africa was still the mysterious 'Dark Continent', and Stanley and Livingstone's historic meeting was a decade into the future. The conditions for picture taking confound belief. He laboured for hours in his wicker dark-room in the sweltering heat of the desert, while the volatile chemicals fizzed dangerously in their trays. Back in London he exhibited his photographs and was 'rapturously cheered' by members of the Royal Society. His reputation as a photographer was made overnight.

By the 1870s the railways had threaded their way across the country, and Bank Holidays and half-day Saturdays had been made obligatory by Act of Parliament. All of a sudden the working man and his family were able to enjoy days out, take holidays, and see a little more of the world.

With typical business acumen, Francis Frith foresaw that these new tourists would enjoy having souvenirs to commemorate their days out. For the next thirty years he travelled the country by train and by pony and trap, producing fine photographs of seaside resorts and beauty spots that were keenly bought by millions of Victorians. These prints were painstakingly pasted into family albums and pored over during the dark nights of winter, rekindling precious memories of summer excursions. Frith's studio was soon supplying retail shops all over the country, and by 1890 F Frith & Co had become the greatest specialist photographic publishing company in the world, with over 2,000 sales outlets, and pioneered the picture postcard.

Francis Frith had died in 1898 at his villa in Cannes, his great project still growing. By 1970 the archive he created contained over a third of a million pictures showing 7,000 British towns and villages.

Frith's legacy to us today is of immense significance and value, for the magnificent archive of evocative photographs he created provides a unique record of change in the cities, towns and villages throughout Britain over a century and more. Frith and his fellow studio photographers revisited locations many times down the years to update their views, compiling for us an enthralling and colourful pageant of British life and character.

We are fortunate that Frith was dedicated to recording the minutiae of everyday life. For it is this sheer wealth of visual data, the painstaking chronicle of changes in dress, transport, street layouts, buildings, housing and landscape that captivates us so much today, offering us a powerful link with the past and with the lives of our ancestors.

Computers have now made it possible for Frith's many thousands of images to be accessed almost instantly. The archive offers every one of us an opportunity to examine the places where we and our families have lived and worked down the years. Its images, depicting our shared past, are now bringing pleasure and enlightenment to millions around the world a century and more after his death. For further information visit: www.francisfrith.co.uk

FREE PRINT OF YOUR CHOICE

Mounted Print
Overall size 14 x 11 inches (355 x 280mm)

**Choose any Frith photograph in this book.
Please note: photographs with a reference
number starting with a "Z" are not Frith
photographs and cannot be supplied under
this offer.**
Simply complete the Voucher opposite and
return it with your remittance for £2.25 (to cover
postage and handling) and we will print the
photograph of your choice in SEPIA (size 11 x 8
inches) and supply it in a cream mount with a
burgundy rule line (overall size 14 x 11 inches).
Offer valid for delivery to one UK address only.

**PLUS: Order additional Mounted Prints
at HALF PRICE - £7.49 each** (normally £14.99)
If you would like to order more Frith prints from
this book, possibly as gifts for friends and family,
you can buy them at half price (with no
additional postage and handling costs).

PLUS: Have your Mounted Prints framed
For an extra £14.95 per print you can have your
mounted print(s) framed in an elegant pol-
ished wood and gilt moulding, overall size 16 x
13 inches (no additional postage and handling
required).

IMPORTANT!

**These special prices are only available if you use
this form to order. You must use the ORIGINAL
VOUCHER on this page (no copies permitted). We
can only despatch to one UK address. This offer
cannot be combined with any other offer.**

Send completed Voucher form to:
**The Francis Frith Collection, Frith's Barn,
Teffont, Salisbury, Wiltshire SP3 5QP**

CHOOSE A PHOTOGRAPH FROM THIS BOOK

Voucher for FREE and Reduced Price Frith Prints

*Please do not photocopy this voucher. Only the original is valid,
so please fill it in, cut it out and return it to us with your order.*

Picture ref no	Page no	Qty	Mounted @ £7.49	Framed + £14.95	Total Cost £
		1	Free of charge*	£	£
			£7.49	£	£
			£7.49	£	£
			£7.49	£	£
			£7.49	£	£
			£7.49	£	£

*Please allow 28 days
for delivery.
Offer available to one
UK address only*

* Post & handling	£2.25
Total Order Cost	£

Title of this book . . . .
I enclose a cheque/postal order for £ . . . .
made payable to 'The Francis Frith Collection'

OR please debit my Mastercard / Visa / Maestro card,
details below

Card Number

Issue No (Maestro only)   Valid from (Maestro)

Expires   Signature

Name Mr/Mrs/Ms . . . .
Address . . . .
. . . .
. . . .
. . . . Postcode . . . .
Daytime Tel No . . . .
Email . . . .

ISBN: 1-84589-219-4   Valid to 31/12/08

FREE PRINT - SEE OVERLEAF

CAN YOU HELP US WITH INFORMATION ABOUT ANY OF THE FRITH PHOTOGRAPHS IN THIS BOOK?

We are gradually compiling an historical record for each of the photographs in the Frith archive. It is always fascinating to find out the names of the people shown in the pictures, as well as insights into the shops, buildings and other features depicted.

If you recognize anyone in the photographs in this book, or if you have information not already included in the author's caption, do let us know. We would love to hear from you, and will try to publish it in future books or articles.

OUR PRODUCTION TEAM

Frith books are produced by a small dedicated team at offices in the converted Grade II listed 18th-century barn at Teffont near Salisbury, illustrated above. Most have worked with the Frith Collection for many years. All have in common one quality: they have a passion for the Frith Collection. The team is constantly expanding, but currently includes:

Paul Baron, Jason Buck, John Buck, Heather Crisp, David Davies, Louis du Mont, Isobel Hall, Lucy Hart, Julian Hight, Peter Horne, James Kinnear, Karen Kinnear, Tina Leary, Stuart Login, Sue Molloy, Miles Murray, Sarah Roberts, Kate Rotondetto, Dean Scource, Eliza Sackett, Terence Sackett, Sandra Sampson, Adrian Sanders, Sandra Sanger, Julia Skinner, Lewis Taylor, Shelley Tolcher, Lorraine Tuck, Miranda Tunnicliffe, David Turner and Ricky Williams.